AGRICULTURAL ADVENTURES 'n GOD

by Jon Liechty

Along with a desire to clearly tell the stories of my life I am aware of a need to protect the privacy of friends, neighbors, colleagues and acquaintances; therefore, I have used alternative names for some. –Jon Liechty

Copyright © 2014 by Jon Liechty
Copyright © 2013 by Jon Liechty
First Edition

All rights reserved. No part of this book shall be reproduced, stored in a retrieval system, or transmitted by any means without written permission from the author.

ISBN: 978-0-692-33598-7

Printed in the United States of America
DxDesign - Carol Dumonceaux - email: carol@dxdesign.biz

Scripture taken from the HOLY BIBLE, NEW INTERNATIONAL VERSION ® . Copyright © 1973, 1978, 1984 by International Bible Society. Used by permission of Zondervan. All rights reserved.

ACKNOWLEDGMENT

My sincere appreciation to all the people who have helped me in this book writing venture.

First of all my wife, Fern, who helped many times with spelling, punctuation, and phraseology. Her continued patience during my times of seclusion and times when I needed complete silence. I know it wasn't always easy. She stayed with me all the way, what a great loving partner.

Without the skills of Paul Freitag assisting in layout pattern, his editorial style and book chapter design, this writing would not have made it. Thank you Paul, what a great friend.

The encouragement of Dan Johnson kept me going. In the early stages of discussing the idea with Dan and his reassurance that I could do it (knowing the family background). Believing that the project was worth while and his projected vision, thank you Dan, what great camaraderie.

And finally the assistance of my secretary, June Werre, for her skills on the computer. When my laptop locked up June knew where to go to get me going again. Also for all the retyping process when time and again I would change the script. Thank you June, what great perfection.

Many thanks to Evelyn Sjostrom, and her professional art skills, for allowing me to place her drawing of the barn, house, and garage on the cover of this book.

Jon Liechty

FORWARD

While many things can be learned from textbooks, sometimes the greatest lessons and principles for life and success come from the life of a person who has walked the journey of life for eight decades. These are the people I love to listen to as they share the stories of what brought them to where they are today. It gives a person a window into decision-making, family values, hard work, inter-personal relationships, finances, spiritual development, ministry, and career development. From these stories, we can learn to appreciate the blessings we have, expand our thinking, appreciate life, celebrate the success of others and laugh with each other.

In this book, my friend Jon Liechty shares the journey of his life. I have known Jon and his family for most of my life. His three children were closer to my age and so I knew them better than Jon. However, I know that the quality of persons that they were was an outgrowth of what they learned from their parents, Jon and Fern. Jon and I had more opportunities to interact because of work with North Central University. Over these years our friendship has grown and we have enjoyed fellowship in a number of settings.

However, I really felt I knew Jon after I read his book, "Out Behind the Barn." It is an honest, straight-forward portrayal of his life that provides a number of insights into what has made him a success in God's eyes. If you read this carefully, you will find numerous principles that will bring joy and meaning to your life. You will learn about faithfulness and consistency. You will learn what it means to be a businessman who uses his resources and life to serve others. You will discover the value of networking. In addition to that, you will be challenged to recognize a point in life that influences every decision you make. For Jon, the meeting took place, "Out Behind the Barn."

What I appreciate about Jon is that he has learned to be flexible and adapt to changes throughout life. He values the past but does not demand that things be done the same way. He probably learned this in farming. He is an entrepreneur who sees how things can be better. However, instead of complaining about it, he gets involved and effects change. There are many things in life that can cause a person to become bitter and critical of people and programs around them. Jon has chosen to enjoy life and adapt to changes around him. He is a person anyone would be blessed to have as a friend, and I am honored to call him my friend.

Dr. Paul A. Freitag
Vice President of Advancement
North Central University

PREFACE

This book may be one of the most important things you have ever done because it shows what God can do with a country boy who works hard, loves the Lord and puts God first. This book is a credit to the gospel, a tribute to your parents and it will be a blessing to your children and children's children as well as to all others who read it. This is a thrilling book; it ought to be widely distributed. It will be an inspiration to those who read it, and most importantly, it will bring glory to God.

Someone once said to me, commenting on my father's life and character, "He was a mark in the land."

The Liechty family has been a "mark in the land"—only eternity will reveal the extent of blessing God has poured through your lives, going back to your mother and father.

Daniel E. Johnson

LIST OF MIRACLES

Silas-Run Over 21
Jonathan-Hay Slide 28
Paul & Jonathan-Skunks 32
Jonathan-Run Away Horses 39
Paul - Scarlet Fever 44
Jonathan-Overheated 45
Adam-US Army 51
Jonathan-US Army 57
Jonathan-US Army 58
Jonathan-Made An Altar 60
No Girl-Got The Farm 68
Jonathan-Bale Hook Accident 69
Ezra-Bull Chase 72
Fern-Wedding 77
Banker-Moves 94
Charles DeLair-Farm 100
Hank DeLair-Farm 100
New Ford-Gave Up 107
Jeffrey-Truck Rollover 139
NCU-Orfield Apts. 143
Howard Dahl-Concord 148
Wesley Loven-Accident 153
Frank Fieberger-Conservation 167
Marilyn Johnson-Yakima 172
Jonathan-Madrid Holdup 174
Selling-Concord Air Seeder 178
Worker Labor-Provided 179

Florida Park-Sale 181
Pioneer Seed-Transfer 185
Jeffrey-Return to Farm 188
Beginning-Minot Sales 190
Farm Expands- Minnesota 191
Bismarck-More Parks 192
God Thing-Mennonite Help 222
Check Surprise-$40,000 227
Colorado-Farm 227
Ben-Material Holdings 230
NCU-Mansion 233
TBC-Fitness Center 235
Youth For Christ-Gym 237
Elsie-Maybe-Yes 238
Chrysler Van-Flying 238
Ignite Light-Headquarters 239
Reward-Financial 241
Cell Phone-Returns 241

TABLE OF CONTENTS

The Early Days 11

Early Teen Years 38

College Days And Army Life 49

Back To The Farm..63

Romance 74

Building A Business...84

The Start Of Special Connections..91

Expanding Real Estate 102

Business And Travel 125

A New Paradigm Of Business..141

Friendships..147

God's Sovereign Protection 153

New Opportunities For Business And Ministries 168

New Leadership 188

Fern's Cookies 194

God's Healing Touch 199

Additional Connections 203

Ever Greatful..242

Grandpa & Grandma
Witmer

Grandpa & Grandma
Liechty

One
THE EARLY DAYS

My parents, John and Clara (Witmer) Liechty, moved to Brinsmade, North Dakota in 1914. Clara moved there with her parents, John and Mary Witmer, along with 35 other people as a group. The group included the Gerigs, Ringenbergs, Witmers, and Ehnerts. John Liechty, from his youth was adventurous, tired of small thinkers, came as a single man along with the group. They chartered a train to haul all their belongings, which included farm machinery, horses, cattle, and their house wares and all living possessions. Moving to North Dakota was a challenge, to say the least, stopping every day to feed and water the cattle and horses. The trip took two weeks. It was believed that Mr. Tom Ose, a realtor who owned a Brinsmade Bank and a Grain Elevator, had persuaded these families to come west to explore new territory.

Roads in North Dakota were very few, and poor at best, suitable only for horses. Sometime later John acquired a motorcycle. John said he could jump over both sets of railroad tracks in Brinsmade, approx 50 feet, in one jump.

John had a team of horses and a buggy to do his courtship with Clara, how far they would drive around town and country is anybody's guess. Brinsmade had a drugstore with a soda fountain. A malt or a shake were only twenty five cents but he only had a nickel in his pocket. He could only stand and drool. The town also had two restaurants, and at least three churches (eventually this Indiana group leaned toward the Christian and Missionary Alliance Church) available to young couple lovers. John commented a few times about the bad odor from the horses as he would haul his sweetheart (Mother) on a date.

John H. Liechty born April 6, 1890 to Peter and Anna Liechty near Ft. Wayne, Indiana, in an Amish home. Peter Liechty ancestry goes back to 1540 in Laudisvil, Switzerland.

John decided to go west and explore new country. Clara May Witmer was born July 20, 1894 near Ft. Wayne, Indiana, in a home where they attended a Church Of God of Anderson, Indiana. Although John and Clara grew up in the same community in Indiana they never met before coming to North Dakota. They were married December 3, 1914 at Minnewaukan, North Dakota. We have no details of the wedding, although we do know the county judge married them.

After marriage they bought a piece of ground six miles from Brinsmade, the closest town, and began building their first one room home. Can you imagine starting with no building, hauling material enough for one room, six miles with horses and wagon? Once you're there, there is no telephone or electricity and what do you do for groceries, milk, water, mail and doctor?

The only part of normalcy to any of this life Dad and Mom started with is the fact that children came along on a kind of normal routine. Adam was born June 25, 1918, Ezra was born March 8, 1921, It was time for Jonathan to be added on July 18, 1926, Clara called out and said "here comes Jonnie". The doctor came, with horse and buggy two hours late, and said you're here already. I said, yes Doc and I'm not going back either. Paul was added to the family November 27, 1927.

While horses have been the source of power for generations back, mechanized horsepower is just coming into being at the start of the 20th century. On September 9th, 1922 the Brinsmade Star wrote about the beauty of the steam engine. It is a combination of mechanical engineering and functional aesthetics. They were thrilled with the hushed sound of that steam engine when they got everything finely adjusted. It was almost silent, but a "moving" silence. With a hot fire, full steam pressure and drain petcocks closed, that engine idled with almost no sound. The balanced flywheel spun on one end of the crankshaft which rotated in journals well oiled with a recent twist of the grease cups. The intake and exhaust valves opened and closed willingly in this symphony of mechanical function. All that motion with the power of 20 horses, and yet you could hear crickets chirping in the distance.

My first memories of school were 4th and 5th grade. I must stop here and say that by this time in school, Dad and Mom had moved to a better farm only two miles from Brinsmade. The good part was it was a lot closer to town, the bad part that it was close enough (two miles to school) that we were able to walk to school every day, unless real bad weather came, then Adam or Dad would take us with the horses and wagon or sleigh. Sleigh trails in the winter were just like road trails. These snow trails would build up and pack hard and would be the last snow to melt in the spring. We could make home made ice cream from the snow and ice. The horses always knew the way home. I remember on cold days we would start the horses for home from school, we'd cover the wagon box with a big canvas and sit under there until the horses stopped at the barn about 40 minutes later. Sometimes the driver would bring along some lunch, or stop at a store and buy some candy, and we would have an under-the-canvas sleigh ride picnic. In the summer time we walked and tried to catch rides with the neighbor kids. Sometimes it worked but most times not. Walking wasn't bad on nice days. We could throw rocks at gophers or try to skip flat rocks on the water across sloughs. Sometimes we carried sling shots and fired at birds and of course we always carried lunch buckets, most likely Karo syrup or jelly sandwiches with maybe a slice of dill pickle, no hot lunches at school. The Mitchell family(two boys, Jack and Billy) drove a big Chrysler sedan and the Olstead family(one girl Margie) drove a Chevy sedan to take their children to school each day and they were our best chances for rides.

Our school was a four-room school in Brinsmade, North Dakota. There were two rooms on the main floor, four grades in each room. Four years of high school and the principals office were upstairs. The basement contained a large coal furnace and huge coal bin, usually full of big lump lignite coal from western North Dakota. The coal was shipped in by rail and hauled to school on bids, which was about 50¢ a ton to shovel off the boxcar and shovel again into the basement. It was a dirty, blackening job to say the least. Horse and wagon hauled the coal.

One of the things I remember about 4th to 6th grade was reading. If there was extra time at the end of the day, or before recess, the teacher would have me read stories to the entire classroom (only one teacher for four grades of school). I never considered myself a reader and still don't read a lot to this day, but my teacher must have thought I was okay. Recesses of course were everything from ball games to playground rides. In high school we played basket ball, but no foot ball. One ride I always enjoyed was called giant strides, which consisted of a high pole in the middle, with a wheel at the top, and chains hanging down that we could hang onto while we'd run in a circle and swing way out. The faster we ran the farther we flew. If we had a fresh snowfall, we played fox and goose. Some of the kids in my class were considered the toughest guys in town. Two different times we almost got into fights. I never really had a fight. I was a friend to everyone. But you know there is always a bully (Dick) in every crowd. Dick had been challenged to fight me. The kids standing by would scream, "Hit him, hit him!" We stood right up to each other, but neither ever swung at the other. I know he could have licked me but I stood right up to him and he never dared swing. Dick was taught at home to fight and we boys weren't allowed to fight.

On one occasion in high school we were scrimmaging in the gym and Dick snuck up behind me when I had the ball in my hands and he hit me a good one on the jaw. I walked off the floor and let him go. Our mother would always say, "The smartest one gives up first!" What great wisdom.

I do remember fun times in school. When I was 12 years old I was able to get a driving permit, the reason being, to help on the farm. The day I went to get my permit I drove to Minneaukan, ten miles away, without a permit, all by myself. Dad told me to go see the County Judge for my permit. The Judge asked me, how did you get here? I said, "I drove". The judge just shook his head, but granted me a driving permit. My first drive on the way home was going past a field where one of my brothers was working. I thought I should wave as I went by and drove right into the ditch, I just turned the wheel and went right back up on the road. Dad would let me drive to school so we kids could get home sooner to help him on the farm. Having a car in school was a prestigious event in those days. Of course it allowed us to have a few boys and maybe girls too, to take up town at noon for a 5¢ bottle of pop or some 1¢ chewing gum. I also remember malts were only 25 cents. On slippery days it just worked out to do a few wheelies with the car. The main center of town had a flagpole, and it seemed as though that 1938 Plymouth wouldn't turn around that pole without a good slide sideways. Then there were times when big brother

Ezra would be driving the car and he would take us out on the lake on ice and there we could really wheel around. He would speed up to forty or fifty miles per hour and let the car go into a slide that went for a quarter of a mile. We had good reasons not to tell Dad. Although Dad had a few good stories to tell, like when they put somebody's buggy out on top of the barn, or loosen a wheel nut so the wheel would fall off or hide some ones horses, take the bridles off and let them hang loose.

In the 7th and 8th grades there were just four of us, two boys and two girls both years. I had a girl in the desk in front of me and one girl beside me. Believe it or not, they both liked me. My brothers thought the girls had poor eyesight. Remember, my mother said I was a pretty baby.

By this time I had to miss a lot of school to help on the farm so some of my classes were hard to keep up. When we would do workbooks, Margie in front of me would hold her book up as though reading it and I would copy some of the answers, Anna would pass me her papers. Was it right? No, but I felt it was all I could do because I had to stay home and work three months out of the nine months of school.

My ninth year in school was different from the norm. By now I was 15 years old. I really missed a lot of school. One of my subjects was English and most of it went pretty well except the book reports. When was I to read a book while working on the farm every evening? Yes, we would get home from school, and Mom would give us some cookies or a rolled up pancake with jelly and some milk to drink to hold us over till supper. We had 20 plus milk cows and we helped milk in the morning and evening before and after school. Sometimes after school I would drive horses in the field till dark pulling a harrow, disc or grain drill.

My English teacher really wanted me to pass my grades. While teaching, she had children at home and kept an in-house babysitter named Evelyn who was 14 years old and dropped out of school. My teacher would have me stop by her house occasionally. That's how I got to know Evelyn. We thought we were in love. My English teacher said Evelyn could read a book, tell me the story, and I could write a book report from that. It worked and I passed my 9th grade English. I remember getting an F on my report card, Dad went to the teacher and said Jonnie didn't deserve that F. The Teacher said, "No, he doesn't" but that is the lowest grade I had. This was in spring of 1941.

Now let me go back and talk about some earlier family and farm life events.

Dad was an entrepreneur in his day. In 1928 he had bought a second farm just south of the home place. When Uncle Levi and Aunt Katie Neuhouser came to North Dakota they moved to that farm. The Neuhousers were a large family. They along with us would visit at one place or the other making home made ice cream. The dirty thirties hit, the dust bowl of the times. High winds with dust in the air, hiding the sun, eroded the soil blowing tumble weeds and ground over fences completely covering fences and filling road ditches level full. The tumble weed, a prickly thistle, grew into a round ball shape plant, about eighteen to twenty two inches in diameter, then after it ripened it would let loose and roll in the wind. Due to hard depression times Dad lost the second farm and in 1935 the Neuhousers moved back to Indiana. However our cousin Darlene was born in North Dakota.

On New Year's day, January 1, 1932, Dad got up at 6 o'clock in the morning and got Adam out of bed. Mom was going to have a baby. "Adam," Dad said, "You need to go get the doctor." None

Adam 19, Ezra 16, Jonathan 11, Paul 10, Silas 5, Reuben & Ruth 2

of us boys knew anything about a baby coming up to this time. Telephone lines were out of working order, some under snow drifts, the old style crank phone that hung on the wall didn't work, roads were blocked with snow, and the only thing left to do was go with a horse. Adam saddled up Beauty, our riding horse, and went to get the family doctor who lived in Brinsmade, two miles away. By the time the doctor got his horse hooked up to the sleigh and came two miles to the farm house, Silas was born. It was New Year's Day. Our closest neighbors, the Ringenbergs, less than a mile away, came to visit. We boys of course didn't know where

Silas came from. Our parents said Ringenbergs brought him and went back home again. Paul and I believed this for several years. We knew nothing about where babies came from by looking at what kind of clothing our mother wore. Mom never hung any of her under clothing on the out door clothesline with the rest of the family wash. There being only boys in the family, we had no idea as to what kind of clothing ladies wore. We boys didn't know that babies were breast-fed.

MIRACLE 1 As long as we're talking about Silas, I remember when Dad was backing the Model T Ford out of the garage. Silas, who was one year and nine months old at the time, was backed over with the back wheel of the Model T. Dad stopped, picked him up, (I saw this with my own eyes) and carried him to the house. I think Dad and Mom's prayers brought him back, they never took him to a doctor. Of course, Silas was always tough, or maybe that's what is wrong with him now!, not really.

Our Dad was real curious about any kind of church activities he heard about, and one of his adventures was to take us to a camp meeting 250 miles from home. I was only seven years old (1933) when Dad hooked our 1926 Model T Ford to a 4-wheel flat top trailer. Mom loaded groceries and bedding for five days supply. What kind of groceries would you take without a refrigerator or a microwave? Dad loaded a tent for sleeping and covered it all with a big tarpaulin and ropes, and off we went to Lake Geneva camp meeting at Alexandria, Minnesota. Adam must have gotten up set, he got up in his sleep, crawled through a fence and went looking for horses. Dad took us fishing early in the mornings. Lake Geneva had a lot of little sunfish that Mom would fry up for lunch. Then Dad with his cap turned side ways and smile on his face would sing:

Bread and fish upon the fire,
Come and fill your heart's desire.

On February 17th, 1935 Reuben and Ruth joined the family. By this time I was old enough to know how they got here, but was still not sure about Silas. When the twins were born, Reuben appeared to be the weaker one of the two. Being born right at home, when we got up in the morning Reuben was in the oven of the kitchen range, a wood and coal burner that had a reservoir tank at one end that kept hot water. I saw that first hand. Mom had put him in there to warm him up. These were two six pound babies, they fit in the palm of our hand. The doctor came out to see mom later.

At that time they did not know Ruth was the weaker of the two. She had an open-heart valve that didn't work right. Her fingers and toes always looked blue. She was a very smart and cute little girl. Mother would sew little dresses, bonnets and clothing for her only girl. She put a lot of ribbons in Ruthie's hair. She was so very proud of her little girl. Mom's only daughter passed away at age 4 ½. This was a big disappointment to our mother. She always kept a positive attitude.

Earlier I mentioned the 1926 Model T Ford, but there was also a 1928 4-door Buick Sedan at the farm, it looked big and prestigious standing beside the model T. The whereabouts or where it came from I never knew. This Buick, big as it was, was very maneuverable with Dad at the wheel. It made many field trips, hauling lunch to farm helpers and threshers. It would pull large grain trailers of wheat from the field to the bin site. Wheat, oats and corn were all shoveled into the granary bins, by hand, using a scoop shovel. This was heavy, hard, sweaty work that put lots of muscle on farm boys. There were no grain augers in those

Model T Ford used to peddle Watkins products 1934-36

days. Dad and the Buick could get the cows and horses home from the pastures and still take us to church on Sunday and mid-week Bible study. Church and Bible study were never missed and there was never farm work on Sundays. One time our big herd bull ran off to Brinsmade and got into another herd of cows. Dad took the big Buick and separated the bull away from the cows by going back and forth and in circles. You cannot imagine the amount of dust and dirt that flew into the air as the tires were spinning and sliding on the grass. People standing by watching said it was the best rodeo ever to come to town. This took place on the Brinsmade Ball Diamond.

The Model T Ford was used, as I remember, by Adam and Ezra to peddle Watkins Products from 1934 to 1936. They went from farm to farm, selling Watkins products, to help make a living for the family. Farmers were far from town and they would buy from them. Watkins vanilla, red lineament, and two different kinds of salve ointments for both man and beast were big sellers.

During these early winter years Dad, in a shop heated by wood and coal, began building a travel trailer. We never knew why he started some projects and what he was thinking but most times things ended up right. In the winter of 1936 he was ready to go. The trailer had a stove and icebox and there was a place for all nine of us to sleep. Dad had made four spring-type beds, in an upper deck fashion, held up by two inch well pipes, for us four oldest boys to sleep on. This was above mom and dad's bed at one end of the camper. It was good we had an open ventilator in the ceiling above us four boys. Mom and dad's bed was a studio couch that we sat on in the daytime. We hooked up the 1934 Chevy Sedan, dad traded the 1926 model T Ford for this four door sedan, and away we went to Indiana to our Grandpa Liechty's farm. This was an Amish type farm. There was no electricity in the house, barn, or else where. They had kerosene lamps in the house and carried railroad type lanterns in the barn. We stayed there until after New Year's. He talked his brother, Uncle Silas, who had also built a

Homemade camper Dad built, went to Florida in 1936 and to California in 1937

travel trailer, into joining him and going to Florida. Uncle Silas's family was eight and we were nine for a party of 17. We were only a few miles from Grandpa's farm when Uncle Silas hit some ice and flipped over his camper, spreading eggs and the oats that he packed the eggs into, all over the inside of the camper. They set the camper back on its wheels and kept going, determined to go on. We over-nighted at gas stations, grocery store lots, parks or whatever looked good. There were no KOA with camper hook ups. Our dad and my uncle were ahead of their times. No one traveled all winter in a 7 X 24 ft. trailer in those days. We did have a 6-volt light system that ran off two car batteries. Our neighbors called us gypsies. We finally landed near Plant City, Florida, the strawberry capital of the world. Dad negotiated with two farmers to pick their strawberries into small one quart size boxes for three cents a quart. They let us park our homemade campers in their farmyards and have access to outdoor privies (toilets).

The picking was ½ day job each day. We worked one day at one farm and the next day at the other farm, alternating every other day. Some days were very warm. Omer, Uncle Silas' son, would lay on the ground to pick berries, some of the rest of us did too. The farmer would call out, "do you want a pillow?"

The afternoons were fun times for two sets of cousins playing softball, volleyball and swimming. Our dads gave us ½ cent per quart of berries we picked for our spending money. The dads got the other 2-½ cents to use for groceries.

We returned back to North Dakota the middle of March 1937. The boys of school age went back to school until the end of school year and everybody pitched in for another year of farming. Nineteen thirty-seven was probably the first good farm year since the depression of the thirties. I don't remember much about the depression. It seemed I grew up working as far back as I could remember, so when better times came it was work as usual, nothing changed. We always milked, 20 cows or more, by hand.

Nineteen thirty-seven being a good year at the farm, 20-bushel wheat yields at near $3.00 a bushel, Dad traded off the 1934 Chevrolet for a new 1937 Dodge 4-door Sedan. Now his roaming fever stirred inside him and away we went to California for the winter of 1937-1938. That winter we parked on a side street right by Angeles Temple. Amie Semple McPherson, founder and pastor, built this large auditorium. This was a large two-balcony church that had meetings every night. Each weekend featured a different illustrated Bible story plus other topics like *Jack and The Beanstalk* or *The Cow Jumped Over The Moon*.

Paul and I were the only boys of school age. Mom and Dad encouraged us to go to the nearest school regardless where we were squatted down and of course the teachers always shook their heads and wondered what we came for. Our school curriculum didn't match theirs, we just were not on the same page. We were never at one school long enough to write a test.

Paul and I made us each a pair of roller boards and passed a lot of time rolling on California sidewalks. Cement sidewalks was something we didn't have in the Brinsmade, North Dakota area. Oh well, we did have some wooden walkways built in the turn of the 19th century, but no cement walkways. Dad, Adam and Ezra picked California oranges to make some money.

When we returned to North Dakota in March 1938, it was farming as usual. One point of interest you might wonder about was what happened to the 20 milk cows during our winter excursions. We had a family friend, Sam Miller, who in the depression of the thirties had really dried out for hay and feed for his cattle and he was willing to bring his cattle to our farm and feed them from our hay and grain. At the same time he would feed our cows, milk and sell the cream for his groceries.

I remember the second year, now March of 1938, Sam prepared to move his cows back home only to find three of his cows missing. Paul and I, in our early teens, got the idea to chase three of his cows up the barn stairway into the hayloft. Many barns only had boards nailed to the wall to climb up on. Our barn had a nice stairway to the hayloft, same as house built stairs, it was easy to get the cows to go up. Sam hunted those cows for two days until he found them upstairs in the hay. Dad also thought it was a good joke.

The big round roof haymow provided a lot of fun for us boys. At certain seasons the hay was all gone and we could swing a length of 50 feet from one end to the other. At times we would tie Shep, our dog, in the ropes and let him swing. He barked and growled and really got mad at times because of the wild ride. Our Dad built this barn, as well as the house, garage, elevator and other buildings. Our Uncle, Adam Witmer, helped build the barn. Adam said Dad would cut a piece of board, on the ground, hand it up to Adam and the piece fit every time. Dad was a very good builder and I can remember when Dad was hired to supervise the large auditorium at Lakewood Park Bible campgrounds.

Dad nursed a flock of tame pigeons in the haymow and once a year we would go up and harvest them. They had a big box at one end where they hatched their young. The box had both inside and outside entrants for the birds. It was fun to listen to their humming and cooing at night. Catching them as they flew around was a challenge and sometimes we got a splatter of poop on the nose or in the eye. When caught these birds were feather picked and dressed ready to cook for the kitchen table.

His eye is on the sparrow.

Look people in the eye.

Floss your teeth.

Have a dog

Life's little instructions

MIRACLE 2 Bad luck prevailed also as I slid head first down off the big hay pile, down through the hole where we put hay down for the horses, landed on my nose as I hit the edge of the manger that the horses were tied to This was serious because my nose was bent 40 degrees to the right. Dad rushed me to Dr. Vigland, the doctor who I'm sure delivered me at birth at the house. He took one look and pushed my nose right back straight. I remember he held up a yardstick as a straight edge to get my nose back in line far enough.

One other event at the barn was jumping off the top of the barn onto a wagon load of hay 20 feet below. One time we threw the dog off the barn into the hay pile. Old Shep was a good sport and always followed us if he could climb the obstacles. Shep had the misfortune of getting one of his hind legs cut up in a mower. It was unbelievable how well he could keep up with us with one stiff leg. Shep would always keep other animals like rabbits, raccoons, weasels, foxes and skunks out of the yard. It was very evident when he tussled with a skunk. Shep was a friend to the whole family. Mother always fed him good food off the table.

There was some mischief in all the boys. While no one ever smoked at our house, we all tried imitations of such. Paul and I being matched closest in age did more things together, one of which was sneaking some coffee and tried rolling cigarettes, trying to smoke them out behind the barn. This of course is not what prompted the title of this book. Continue reading, that will come later.

Big barn we often played in also 41 Buick mentioned in book.

The two dogs we all played with.

Sunday was always a relaxing day because we didn't work in the fields. However, the 20 milk cows had to be fed and milked. Dad and Mom had company for Sunday dinner real often. They usually invited people from the church, which included Mr. and

Mrs. G. L. Riffe. At milking time it was a real pain to leave company at the house and go milk cows. Our mother would come to us boys and talk real soft and say nice things to get us to go to the barn. The Riffes being there many times, later in life asked me, "What did your mother tell you boys to get you to go milking?" Mrs. Riffe thought our mom had a magic touch to get us going. The Riffes will be picked up again later in this book.

Remember the Sabbath day to keep it holy.
Be forgiving of yourself and others.
Commit yourself to constant improvement.
Make new friends but cherish the old ones.
Take responsibility for every area of your life.
Be there when people need you.
Treat everyone you meet like you want to be treated.
Life's Little Instructions

By this time Paul and I were 12 to 14 years old and still up to tricks! As we were looking for entertainment, one thing we enjoyed was driving the tractors. Paul and I always got stuck with driving the horses in the field while Adam and Ezra got to drive the two tractors because they were older, when actually the horses were a lot more dangerous to work with than the tractors. So we would watch for times when only he and I with Silas and Reuben were home. We would start up the tractors and drive around the yard in a circle for about an hour. Afterwards we would wonder what we could do to cover up the tracks left on the ground. We decided on garden rakes and hoes to cover them and hope it might rain so Dad couldn't see what we did.

Paul and I built a house on wheels, carried by an old wagon, that we took camping to a vacant farmstead a quarter mile away. Besides sleeping in there we had water, crackers, and candy. Our couch in the camper was the seat out of an old worn out car. Mom wouldn't let us cook because of fire danger.

We had one young man work for us. He drove his dad's car to work each day. He called the car, "The Big Plymouth." He would come into the yard at high speeds and do two or three wheelies. The dust, rocks, straw or whatever, would fill the air. It took several minutes for things to settle down. We boys would tell him, "That 'Big Plymouth' sure has got the power!" This would bring on additional speed and circles with the "Big Plymouth."

We told another one of our men to oil the teeth on the harrow because it would make it pull easier, making him think it would be easier on the horses he was driving. With his Scandinavian brogue, the man would say, "truts, truts, notin but." Another thing we did was slip in and untie the horses quietly so they didn't know it. Then we'd get the dog barking in the barn, pound on the wall, and watch all twelve horses go out of the barn at one time. Dad would ask, "What is wrong with the horses?" Another barn trick was to see who could squirt milk the farthest from the cow's teat or try to feed the cats by squirting milk at them as the cats stood out in the aisle. The dog didn't like it so he would stand and bark. Milking cows was another fiasco. We had some cows that were kickers who needed to be hobbled to milk. I don't know why dad could sit down to milk and the cow stood still but for us boys the cow would kick.

During the ages of 12 to 18 we needed some spending money. We had to make our own. A lot of our money was made by hunting and trapping. We would trap fox, shoot Jack Rabbits and pull skunks out of culverts and from under old vacant houses. We retrieved as many as 17 skunks from under one old house. Working in the basement of the house the skunk squirt odor got so heavy we would need to go outside to cough, one time Ezra threw up it was so bad. Skunk hides were worth about two dollars each, so to us boys we were really in the money. Sometimes our hunts got pretty wild. I remember going with the Grasser boys to run after fox. They took their dad's truck and Paul and I were in the back leaning over the cab trying to shoot going 30 miles an hour over rough fields. On these chases we basically only got our guns emptied. Our shots went everywhere except on our target. The drivers didn't stop for gates, fences or rock piles. All they knew was to floorboard the throttle. I hope Mr. Grasser didn't think that Paul and I wrecked his truck.

MIRACLE 3 One time Paul and I were pulling skunks from a culvert, Paul at one end and I at the other. I got excited and shot at a skunk in the culvert and the bullet ricocheted through the culvert and landed in Paul's hand between his thumb and first finger. Dr. Vigland removed the bullet and sewed his hand back together. I cried for two days and thought how badly I would feel if I had killed him.

Another way us boys collected our spending money, after harvest and threshing, Dad would let us take horses and a hay rake out in the wheat fields and we would rake the loose grain into piles. Then we would load the piles of grain into wagons and haul to the threshing machine. We got to keep the money from the wheat we sold.

Another way was to hunt crows and gophers. At the county fair they would pay a bounty for gopher tails and crows legs. As far back as Saturday, July 4th, 1914, the Brinsmade Star announced having GOPHER DAYS. That day Harvey Herman was announced winner of the contest bringing in over 2000 gopher tails. That's how the celebration began. The country side is over run with yellow gophers. They dig up young plants in the field, eat grain before it can be harvested, dig holes and burrows everywhere. A few years earlier, North Dakota began offering a bounty of a penny for every tail they could bring to the Court House. These animals were real pests to farmers in the recession of the dirty thirties. Gophers were everywhere, seemed to increase faster than any good crops would grow in the dust of the dry years. Crows were very hard on pheasant, partridge and prairie chicken nests. Crows would destroy the nests, eat the eggs, and the little birds if they were hatched. A 5-cent bounty was paid for each pair of crow legs.

Then too, we would walk road ditches looking for empty beer bottles. These bottles where worth five to twenty five cents each. There were no, no litter laws, back in them days.

Gopher days at Brinsmade also included a horse pulling contest. I love to watch horses pull! There is probably nothing more beautiful than a well matched pair of draft horses at full draw force – percherons especially. All horses love to run, but draft horses love to pull. Necks arched, heads down, every muscle taut, both beasts pulling equally on the traces. With the driver whistling, yelling and slapping the reigns, they seem to pull for the sake of pulling, for the challenge.

Leave everything a little better than you found it.
Plant a tree on your birthday.
Plant flowers every spring.
Life's Little Instructions

During this period of our age, Dad and Mom were really involved in supporting and working with the church ministry. It seemed as though we kept all the traveling evangelists and pastors at our house. Some stayed a few days while others stayed a few months. Some of them would sit on the couch all day waiting for The Spirit to move them. We had fun with most of them, but the preachers always tried to convert us boys. We were expected to be up at the altar every meeting. I'm sure it was good for us, but it got to be routine and we'd lose the impact.

We would do most anything for a laugh. In those days we had only outdoor toilets. Many where only what you call a one holler. Ours was a three holler, two holes for adults and a third hole for children, having a privacy wall between the two adult holes. Dad had built this to only occupy one half of the building, the other half was a mouse proof part to store food, flour, clothing, etc. It also made a good deep freeze for winter time. We would watch when one or more lady preachers went into the biff and we would throw rocks at the building, keeping them in the toilet till we quit bombarding the walls. The outhouse had open lattice boards on the back side with a place to put sticks through the back wall and rattle paper or whatever was down in the hole. Sometimes a garter snake would get into the hole of the toilet, slither around on the paper and maybe climb the mound, making the necessity of the toilet, short order. An older addition, of the Sears or Wards catalog, were standard paper for the toilet.

Candice and Eliza attended our church. Dad and Mom took them under their wing and they spent a lot of time at our house. They had gained the name of "Old Ladies" by most all people. This was because of the long full skirt dresses they wore. We boys referred to them as paratroopers. We would most generally pick them up for church.

At this time we had a 1941 Buick with electric windows. Silas would pick up the ladies for church, and as they were riding along, he would pop open different windows up and down. The two ladies thought it was the Holy Ghost opening the windows. They really got the victory!

A lady from California, Mrs. Mathews, would call us boys "roosters" and would come around the table and put her hands on us. We really hated that. She was known as Big Emma. Emma would hardly ever eat at the table with the rest of us. She always ate later. Her husband, Vic, was a little skinny man. He had oil investments in California. Vic was very conservative, never offering any help with expenses.

One Sunday after church we went to Frank and Francis Harris' place for dinner. Frank was a great sheep man and always had lots of them around. These people had a pretty daughter, Ruth. Paul always thought he was going with her. Then they would try to hook me up with La Verne Lass. It was a good idea, but nothing ever became of that deal. These were two young church girls that we thought needed dates.

This was in the 30s, the weather was dry and Frank showed us how the grasshoppers were eating up his yard fence. Grasshoppers were everywhere. They would fly in droves like clouds in the sky. Grasshoppers flourish best in dry hot weather.

That same day Adam was driving on the way home when a tire blew out and we rolled over an almost new 1937 Dodge. No one was hurt. We set the Dodge back up on all four and drove home. That evening we went back to church in a banged up car. A rolled over car wouldn't stop Dad from going to church.

Some of our Sunday afternoons where spent playing softball, riding bicycles, hiking through grain fields and in the wintertime we played in the snow with sleds and skis and made snow houses. We would dig caves out of huge snow piles. We had a lot of fun playing on high straw piles made by the threshing machine during harvest. Dad had built a sheep barn by putting poles in the ground, over laying the poles with fence wire and chicken netting, then threshing straw over top making a huge big straw pile to keep the sheep warm during lambing time. We often played on and rolled off the straw.

In the winter time we would make ice for the next summer. We made a rectangular wall out of straw bails. Each day we poured water on top of water from the day before letting it freeze over night. We kept adding water each day until we had a four foot square cube of ice. The ice was then covered with straw, preferably flax straw, two or three ft. deep. In the summer time we would go chop off a chunk of ice when needed. We needed ice to make homemade ice cream, this was a big hit in summer time.

Our Dad wasn't much for playing softball, horseshoe, hiking or for that matter, any kind of game. He did like hunting and fishing. In the summertime between seeding and harvest he would take us boys down to the Cheyenne River to fish for bullheads and cattails. They were both muddy tasting fish.

In September he always carried his twelve gage Remington pump gun to go after pheasants and partridges. We would get to go along to be his hunting dogs. Dad was a good shot with a gun.

Each year after the first snowfall, usually in November, Dad would take us cottontail hunting. This was in the Silver Lake area. He would find an opening somewhere in the trees, ask us boys to go through the trees and brush and chase the rabbits to him. We would take them home, dress them out and freeze them, until a later time to eat them.

In later years, in Florida, you often found Dad and Mom sitting on a bridge, with their fish poles in hand, maybe one watching while the other one slept. Dad also enjoyed deep sea fishing. He mounted a few nice trophies.

Mom enjoyed playing table games with us boys or reading us stories. Seemed like most of her spare time was used up sewing and knitting. She had a knitting machine that could make gloves, mittens, socks and caps. Then of course, cooking for a large family took a lot of her time. She knew how to season food. Every thing always tasted good. In these days we always had a common drinking dipper for the whole family dipping water out of the same bucket, everyone drinking from the same dipper. Water was carried in from a well by the barn. We didn't waist water.

Two
EARLY TEEN YEARS

By the time I was 15 I had completed my one-year of high school. Dad gave all six boys each one year of high school and then had us stay home to help on the farm. I got room and board (Mom's good cooking) and a car to drive to necessary things, but no wages. All six boys worked at home until they were 21 years old. Dad, having a large farm, always had hired men. This made opportunity to have fun and enjoy working.

As I said earlier, Adam and Ezra got to drive tractors so Paul and I drove horses. Driving horses was much different then driving a tractor, all you do is hit the starter and away you go. First of all the horses needed breakfast, a bucket of oats or ground up mixed feed. Now they needed a drink of water, the only water they got till noon, five hours later. Now you curry the horse down by brushing and raking his fur and relaxing his muscles. Next you began installing the collar, and then the harness, and last of all, the bridle. Now you do this four or six times and finally you have a team ready for work. Then you need to hook them up to a piece of equipment. There is a steering pole to hitch to the collar of the two horses in the middle. You still have the tugs, two on each horse, left to fasten to the evener of various styles on the equipment. Now if the flies weren't too bad that the horse didn't step over the tug and you had the reins in your hand you are ready to go. I did harrowing, plowing, seeding, mowing and raking hay, plus, cutting wheat with binder and four horses. There were times when farmers would hook as many as twelve horses together to pull one disc or plow or cultivator, hooked in tandem, six in front of the other six.

My horse driving experiences were not very good. With five horses on the harrow I had to walk behind all day long for many 10 hour days. The horses knew I was a kid and I just couldn't make them go fast enough. Dad would come out to the field and he could really get them going so fast, I had to run to keep up. Then when he left the field the horses slowed way down again. Dad would say, "Get'em goin," but I couldn't. When I had horses on the mower, I stopped to clean the sickle. Just then the horses stepped forward making the sickle move and cut a piece of my thumb out. I was about one mile from home, but just across from Art Tangelien's, our neighbor's house. They telephoned my parents who came and got me and patched up my thumb. Many a time I had runaways with the hay rake and bundle wagon. The horses would just take off.

MIRACLE 4 The summer I was 15, Dad thought I was a reliable driver. He bought a new John Deere binder pulled by four horses to cut wheat and make bundles for threshing. Dad sent me out about a mile away with the outfit. I was going along pretty good. I got off the binder to put on a chain that had slipped off. All of a sudden, something scared the horses and they took off as fast as they could pull the binder. Of course the binder was set in the motion position, as the horses ran faster all the moving parts like the sickle, gears, chains, and the big reel that pushed the grain onto the platform, these parts got into high velocity speed, throwing some off and breaking others. There was only one problem and that was the gate they went through, going home, wasn't wide enough. The horses got through, but the poor new binder hooked on the big corner post and busted everything in pieces. The horses broke loose and went home on a dead gallop.

When Dad saw the horses come home he wondered what

might have happened to me. Did I get run over? Was I still alive or was I cut in pieces? Dad and Mom both came out to meet me and needless to say, I never saw them happier. They weren't concerned about the binder, just happy to know that I didn't get a scratch. There wasn't much said the rest of the day, but that was the end of my horse driving. "I HATED HORSES – DID I EVER HATE HORSES!" Poor Dad had to repair the binder. He was good at blacksmithing and repairing. I remember seeing him make bearings, out iron and wire and maybe some bolts, when you couldn't buy them. We had one mean horse named Frank. He would stand by the barn door and would not move so I could get in to do chores. Dad didn't believe it, but that horse gave me fits.

As time went on the horse farming disappeared and Dad bought more tractors. One time he had five Case tractors, each one a different model to fit a particular job. Two of our cousins were from Brinsmade. They would come out to play with us and help work if Dad needed help. Dad put one of the boys on a tractor to pull the disc. It had no carriage wheels and therefore going in and out of the fields the disc blades rolled on the ground in a neutral position, not cutting or disturbing grass or soil. The driver forgot to change the angle of the blades when he got to the field and drove over the entire field, doing absolutely no good. We teased him about that.

The other boy was sent out to harrow a field that was planted to wheat. The wooden boss harrow laid flat on the ground. We started him out at four miles an hour, he maintained that speed till he finished the field, not knowing you don't go any faster coming back to the farm with that type of equipment. He put the tractor in road gear, 15 miles an hour. Dirt and rocks and wood filled the air, the harrow got a ride of a lifetime.

One young man came up from Jamestown to work for a week. The second day as he brought the tractor in from the field, from work, he forgot to slow the tractor down as he approached the yard and ran over the big upright gas pump. Knocked it down, breaking it off, flat to the ground. Dad said, "that is city guys for you".

By the end of this summer, in time to haul the wheat bundles in to thresh out the grain and put the straw up in big stacks, Dad made me machine oiler, greaser, light maintenance and belt tightener man. The equipment in those days didn't have sealed grease bearings, and therefore needed oil and grease every hour. This was a great move up for me and I really liked it. Kind of got me started on a route towards the new methods of combines that were just emerging at that time. Working with Dad around the thresher gave me good mechanical experience. The switch from threshing to combining had not taken place yet. Dad was determined at that time he never would make the change.

Harvest and threshing was always an exciting time of the year. It was a time when everybody could get involved in kind of a fun time. For one thing, you were never alone to do the work. Binding the grain into bundles and then standing the bundles on end to make a shock always took two to four people to do the work. It took six bundle teams to bring in the shocked grain to the thresher. It was a time of year when our cousins from Indiana would come out to help work. Cousins like Jessie Liechty, Robert Liechty, Ralph and Delilah Seiler, Velma and Dutch Klauffenstein, Bill Witmer, Merle and Eddie Neuhauser would all get involved.

There was never a dull moment with all these guys. When it rained, they tried to ride and break horses or fix up old cars. One rainy day when we couldn't thresh, Jessie saddled up one of Dads horses. This horse had never been ridden, was wild and rough to handle. Jessie was the star of the show. That horse bucked up and down, two feet off the ground. Jessie hung on to the end, the horse quit bucking, and became a nice riding horse.

Threshing time got Mom involved too. We had 10 to 12 hired men to make a full crew. Mom had to work very hard to feed the men and us boys. She always had a hired girl, Violet Palmer Abrahamson, to help her. Violet was hard working and a great friend of the family. She fit in very well. She helped Mom 18 to 20 years. Some of us boys always helped Mom as well and it was long hours. Dad was a custom thresher. In other words, he moved the thresher from one neighbor to the next to thresh their grains. Sometimes they moved a cook car along and made meals out in the field. That old 1928 4door sedan Buick was the main transportation for Mom and Violet to go from home base to the cook car or the field with coffee and lunches. The cook car, on wheels, was equipped with a stove, a sink, a water tank and a table long enough to seat 15 to 20 people. It had no refrigerator. I don't know how they kept food from spoiling. The cook car was moved from one work site to another with a team of horses or hooked onto the steam threshing rig. Threshing with a steam engine took a lot of man power. You needed a water boy and a man to keep the burner full of straw or coal. Dad had two steamers for farm work. I remember trying to plow with a steam engine pulling an eight bottom plow. The plow was put in and out of the ground by hand, two gangs on one lever. You needed two men on the plow just for that. The engine needed a fireman and a water boy. Traveling only three miles an hour you didn't get much plowed in a day.

Before I leave this time of my life, I want to talk about our family life. We were definitely raised in a Christian home. As early as I can remember, going to church twice on Sunday and

Bible study Wednesday nights, was a must. And then any revival or evangelistic meetings, within a 100 mile radius, had to be explored also. There were monthly fellowship meetings with other churches from a large area that we took in. We would even sing quartet songs at those meetings. Dad, our pastor Herman Kesler, Ezra and I were called quite often to sing. Our Mother played the piano. Then there was a small church, Christian Missionary Alliance at Brinsmade, where Ezra and I sang with George Herman Jr. and our Uncle Adam Witmer, Moms brother, in a quartet. We sang at public school programs, PTA and youth programs.

Go to church Sunday.

Sing in a choir.

Always accept an outstretched hand.

Rekindle old friendships.

Stop blaming others.

Wear polished shoes.

Life's little instructions.

A highlight for us boys was the summer family Bible Camp at Lakewood Park, (near Devils Lake city and on Devils Lake proper) North Dakota. This camp began back in 1935 or 1936. If we stayed overnight, we slept in tents, sleeping bags and blankets. Washrooms and bathrooms were not the greatest. In early 1940-45, Dad and Mom ran the camp store that had all kinds of groceries, ice cream and pop. Coming out of the 1930s Great Depression we had very little ice cream and candy. This was our chance to make that up. Paul and I were able to help at the store and we really had fun with that. It helped us get acquainted with lots of young people. One bad thing was camp only lasted two weeks each summer and we wanted more, especially when we got old enough to drive Dad's new cars and fill them up with girls and some boys. I well remember being jealous of the Herman Johnson boys. They were sons of the Superintendent of the North Dakota District of the Assemblies of God. These boys got first pick of the girls. The rest of us got girls after them. One night we had a load of mixed kids, I was driving 50 miles an hour, someone reached over and turned off the ignition key, when they turned it back on, the muffler was over loaded with gas, it exploded and made a big hole in the muffler of Dads new Plymouth car.

Dad had some trouble at camp meetings with us boys. Always some one of us boys would be missing when it was time to go home. We always went back to the farm at night, 25 miles away. One night one of us boys was missing too long so Dad said we'd go home without him. He started walking home. I'm sure Dad never slept that night. Adam got up and went to meet him about half way home at 9AM. Those girls were always chasing us boys, at least that is what we told Mom and Dad.

Before I leave this part I want to say that every morning at breakfast Dad would read a chapter out of the Bible and pray. It didn't matter how many men were sitting around the table. They had to listen till Dad was done before they could eat. Some of these fellows came into town riding on top of a train of boxcars, they were classified as bums, they slept out in the hay barn. A few fellows thought it was too much religion and quit on the job. However, some of the fellows liked our way of doing things and would come back year after year for harvest season. I remember Louis coming back many years, Herman was another one. And then there was Criss Graber, he got mad at Ezra. Criss was so driver in his automobile. One time Ezra took dads car and pushed Criss's car faster on the road. Criss up and left the farm.

MIRACLE 5 Dad and Mom always prayed for us boys. When

Paul contacted scarlet fever, he was deadly sick and had such a high fever. He could easily have had brain damage or even died. I saw Dad and Mom go to Paul's bed and pray over him. The fever left and he began feeling better each day.

MIRACLE 6 In my case, I had gotten overheated in the school gym, went out in cold weather, cooled off too fast and contacted inflammatory rheumatism. The doctor said I had done damage to my heart. Mom put me in a special bed in our living room where I lay several days. The doctor said I would be laid up for six months. Dad and Mom began praying for me and in two weeks I was out of bed, and back to school within a month. The doctor said at that time I would never be any good for the Army.

Dad and Mom were very reserved around us boys. I never saw them hug or kiss in my whole life. We don't know what went on in the bedroom. We boys often asked how they came up with six boys and a girl. I always felt loved at home. Dad thought the word LOVE sounded fresh, today we use the term sexy. My Dad never told me he loved or liked me, but I never got a spanking from my Dad or Mother. Mom played games with us, but Dad was always busy writing or reading. He sat at a desk, in front of the east window of the living room, by the hour. He would design wall mottos, gospel tracts, and stamps and stickers to put on envelopes. He spent a lot of time preparing sermons in case the opportunity came by.

I don't remember ever being short of food, even in the depression of the 30s. We always had good meals and Mom made lots of variety of foods. If mom wanted chicken for dinner we took a string and the hatchet, went to the chicken coop, picked out a chicken, tied a string around its neck, mom would hold the legs and the wings of the bird. I pulled the string with one hand and cut off its head with my other hand. After the chicken was done flopping around we put him in scalding hot water and picked off the feathers We had a big garden and 20 milk cows. Once a year Dad loaded up wheat from the bin, went to town and ground our own wheat at the mill for flour. We also had a 50-gallon barrel of frozen fish. No kidding, each winter Dad would buy a big 50-gallon barrel of Northern Pike fish that we could eat all winter with home canned vegetables and we also had home canned meats. By spring, the fish were all gone. We ate homemade cheese, popcorn and homemade ice cream all year long. We never went to bed hungry. Mom had a large swing table in the basement suspended from the ceiling by wires. This was a mouse free table where she stored cheese, cakes, pies and other good stuff. They also kept a year supply of potatoes in the basement. A good portion of our diet was corn meal mush. Mom cooked it like hot cereal for the evening meal, put some of it into bread loaf pans, let it set over night to stiffen, then slice and fry it for breakfast, man was it good..

 The main floor of our house consisted of a large kitchen with coal and wood range, a large round table and chairs and kitchen cupboards. The main floor had a large living room with a coal burning heater, sofa and chairs, piano, book case and writing desk, with nice carpet on the floor. We had a bath room with a tub but not a stool and no running water, a utility room with a cream separator and wash sink, also an entry way with a washing machine. Dad always wanted running water, he worked at it until he finally had six boys running after water from the barn to the house.

 Behind our house we only had half neighbors, only the top half. There were no doors between, we only seen them through the windows. We thought they were busts.

 The Brinsmade Star reported we also had electricity installed through out the farm and in 1932 John and Clara were pleased with their new 32 volt system. The Delco plant is nothing more than a one-cylinder, 4 cycle gasoline coupled to a 32-volt electric generator. The generator is connected to a series of 16 wet batteries. The batteries are connected, through a fuse panel, to wires that go to the house, garage, barn, elevator, chicken coupe, and yard light. We had a 32 volt light bulb in every room of the house. Mom ordered a 32 volt washing machine from the monkey's catalog. Every evening about sundown, someone went down into the basement of the car garage, and cranked the Delco plant, until it started.

Some of the farms up by Leeds ND are putting in wind generators instead of gasoline engines. If there is no wind, there is no electricity.

On June 6, 1940, our Dad turned 50 years of age. We had a large celebration. Neighbors from the Brinsmade Christian and Missionary Alliance Church and members of the Minnewauken Union Gospel Tabernacle, including Pastor Herman Kesler, all came to the 50 year event. We made two large freezers of homemade ice cream. There were cakes, pies and sandwiches. It just seemed like Dad was really old. Wow, 50 years and I was 14 at that time. As a boy, Dad looked old to me. I never ever saw our Dad use tobacco or alcoholic beverage.

Drafted into regular Army February 6, 1945

Three
COLLEGE DAYS AND ARMY LIFE

At age 16 1/2, in January 1943 I went to Minneapolis and enrolled at North Central Bible College. Back at that time colleges took students without a high school diploma. My brother Ezra was there in his senior year. I enjoyed this time in college, although beginning at the middle of the year I felt a little lost among a group of 400 students.

It was easy to make friends. We went out on weekends to various churches to help with meetings and to sing in groups from school. When I was in school, classes only went to noon. I got a job for afternoons working for the Minneapolis Street Car Company. My job was to be detective and watch how the conductors did business. Each streetcar had a driver and a conductor who would collect money when people got on to ride. I would get on and ride as a regular passenger and watch if the conductor put the people's money in the jar or if he stuck some in his pocket. I also reported how courteous he would be. It was fun. I'd get on at a certain point and ride 20 to 40 minutes, get off, and walk a few blocks to another route and go that way to some other point in town.

In those days there were 5¢ hamburgers and a bowl of baked beans for 5¢ at the White Castle. Everything else being in perception, I enjoyed Minneapolis.

Our school had an ushering team for some downtown boxing matches. I got in on a few of them. We also took class trips around town and to out-of-town churches. Some Saturdays a group of us students would go to the city park or maybe the zoo and stroll around for exercise. Sometimes in the group we'd be kind of halfway on a date. We tried to abide by the school rules.

Freshmen could only date a girl once a month.

Ezra graduated from North Central Bible College that spring, married a classmate, Marguerite Edlund, and left home to go farming on his own. Adam went to live with his uncles and aunts in Indiana, leaving me the oldest one to help Dad on the farm. I never went back to school. I stayed home and helped Dad on the farm. The winter of 1944 was interesting, Mom and Dad hooked to their camper and drove to Orange, Texas. This was the second camper that Dad built. It had more style and aero-dynamics than the first one he built. Paul, Silas, Reuben, and me, where along on the trip as well. This was War time. Dad got a superintendent job in the shipyards building warships. Paul and I worked other jobs. The government had a national tire rationing system in place. My job was to inspect tires, during the war years you couldn't buy a new tire without an inspection. We had to dismount the tire from the wheel, reverse the tire and mount it back on the wheel again. This was done periodically according to government standards. I also worked in a grocery store a short time, I candied eggs. With

Second camper Dad built, spent winters of 41-42 in Orange, Texas.
Dad worked in ship yards, I worked at gas station and grocery store.

a powerful light you could see through the egg to determine if there might be a bird in the egg. The sign up front in the store said "FRESH YARD EGGS", but occasionally I thought I saw something bad in the egg shell.

MIRACLE 7 September 8th, 1943 my brother Adam was drafted into the US Army. He was married to Marcella, they had their first child, Anita. Adam was in the roughest of battles including the Battle of the Bulge. He had several narrow escapes, one of witch I would like to include here and he quotes;

The time I believe our answer to prayer was most evident, was during the Battle of the Bulge. We had set up our command post in the basement of a house. The company commander came to me and said, we are completely surrounded by the German Army and unless God helps us we are doomed. Then the commander said, I have seen you read your Bible, would you read something and have prayer asking God to help us. Adam said sure, I would be glad to do that. He opened to the 91st Psalm, verses 7 and 8 say, a thousand shall fall at thy side and ten thousand at thy right hand, but it shall not come nigh thee. Only with thine eyes you will behold and see the reward of the wicked. After reading this entire Psalm and having prayer it seemed the shelling ceased. I don't know why, except for prayer, a few hours later all 35 men in that basement got out of there alive. The rest of our Company of 250 men where either captured or killed. Only the 35 men in that basement got out of there alive. You can say what you want, but I believe God heard and answered our prayer that day. The Testament Adam read from that day was given to him by a Gideon at the induction center. Adam received both a Bronze Star and the Purple Heart for outstanding service.

It is the VETERAN who serves under the flag.

It is the VETERAN, not the preacher,
Who gives us freedom of religion.
It is the VETERAN, not the reporter,
Who has given us freedom of the press.
It is the VETERAN, not the poet,
Who has given us freedom of speech.
It is the VETERAN, not the campus organizer,
Who has given us freedom to assemble.
It is the VETERAN, not the lawyer,
Who has given us the right to a fair trial.
It is the VETERAN, not the politician,
Who has given us the right to vote.
It is the VETERAN, who salutes the Flag.

Dad tried to get a farm deferment from the military for me in the summer of 1944 but the draft board said Dad still had three more sons at home. I was drafted into the regular Army on February 6, 1945.

I had my basic training at Fort Lewis, Washington. Fort Lewis is one of the older camps in the country that had been fixed up real nice. We had good warm barracks to sleep in. Training grounds were good. Temperatures in the summer time were cool for drill practice and 10 to 20 mile hikes. At this particular time the United States was drafting men up to 45 years old, many with families at home. Some of the guys were too heavy while others had bad feet and knees. When these guys were on long hikes they just couldn't make it. Ambulances followed us to pick up the fallouts. We all had our turn at K.P. I didn't mind it. It was a chance to get away from the drill sergeants. We stood a lot of reveille and also barrack inspections. One day after I had been in training for six months, the company commander called us to stand inspection. He told me to shave the fuzz off my face. Even at 18½ years of age, I had never shaved.

While in boot camp I met Marvin Clarkson, who became a life long friend. We normally had Saturday and Sunday off unless we were on K.P. Marvin and I would travel to Christian Service Men's Centers. There was one in Seattle and one in Tacoma. These were real good places for clean young soldiers to go. They had beds for over night and lots of finger food, which was all free. They had Christian movies and we could sign up to do church projects if we wanted to go.

Getting off on weekends didn't always go so good. We had barrack inspection at random times and there would always be someone to spoil it. We had one guy, Pvt. Green, he never got his act together. He would leave his towel hang out, or he had mud in his shoes, or his bed wasn't made right. If any one guy goofed up, the whole barracks would be gigged. Nobody from that barracks could leave the base all weekend. Some guys would get so mad they put Green under the shower. I think the poor guy just didn't have it all upstairs. He really should not have been drafted. If you got caught sleeping on guard duty, you could wind up on KP for several week-ends or you may be put to digging a hole in the ground and pushing it shut again.

One weekend we tried hitchhiking to Caldwell, Idaho, which was Marvin's hometown. He said he knew a girl there I should meet. This was on a holiday so we had a three-day pass. We planned one day going, one day there and one day back. It didn't work. We got half way there by noon the second day and decided we had better head back. Connections for hitchhiking were no good that weekend. We got back early in the morning just in time to stand reveille.

Our basic training seemed to go on forever. We finally discovered that the shipping orders for ten of us got laid up on top of a file and forgotten. We began in Fort Lewis early February and were still there when I went home on furlough in August. Although I know someone had to go fight the enemy, I feel the Lord had something else for me. Ten of us were held back in Fort Lewis three and one half months, after basic training, with no destination in sight. Trainees usually got shipped out right after basic.

While I was home on furlough I had the opportunity to be baptized. I had never been immersed in water for baptism. I was able join a group at a lake near Rugby, North Dakota. I do feel according to the Bible being completely immersed is the proper way.

You may remember the war in Europe ended in May, and while I was home in August, Japan surrendered. This was a great day in all of American lives. After furlough going back to camp they finally shipped us out to Camp Beal in California thinking we would go to the Pacific. We stayed there in Camp Beal until December when we were loaded on a troop train for Newark, New Jersey harbor. There we were loaded on a troop ship to sail the Atlantic. Surprising enough Marvin got on the ship too. We sailed fourteen days to LaHarve, France. Eleven of those days I spent feeding the fish. You needed a good stomach as you stood at the chow table. There were no chairs, which meant standing in a line with 20 to 30 other GI's, and when the guy next to you or standing across from you, lost his lunch, I was bound to lose mine too. It wasn't any better down in the sleeping hull. Fourteen hundred of us were stacked six high on canvas bunks. The best bunk was the top, anything lower you may get bombed on. That was the worst sickness I ever went through, It lasted till I got my feet back on the ground.

At LaHarve, France we embarked and loaded on a train named "40 and 8." Here is where Marvin and I got separated. Marvin went to Berlin and I was shipped to Austria. We said good-by not knowing if we would ever see each other again. The ride lasted five days across France and Germany into Austria. This was a cold ride. The "40 and 8s" were just plain boxcars like you ship wheat or coal in, no chairs and no beds or heat. This was in December with temperatures around the zero mark. They let us off once every 12 hours for food and bathroom.

Army Ambulance used to pick up wounded. Also used on weekends to haul skiers up the mountain in Austria.

I was assigned to an ambulance battalion in a small town in Austria. The battalion, made up of 120 ambulances, was divided into four companies. I was assigned as driver in one of the companies. We covered the area taking sick people to hospitals and were on call in case of accidents on the highways. We spent time in the motor pool servicing trucks and jeeps as well as the units we drove. We were really an occupational army service.

This was wintertime with lots of snow and ice, and it was real convenient for skiing on the mountain slopes of Austria. The 4-wheel-drive ambulance would haul us up and we'd ski down at least one half mile.

Being in Austria on Christmas Eve, I attended a Yuletide service in a large Catholic Cathedral, the only church in that small village. Christmas day was just another day, except we had real turkey for dinner.

When springtime came they moved me to Battalion headquarters up at Hamburg, Germany. My assignment was still the same upon arrival. Being there a few days our company commander, a captain, had a jeep that the mechanics of the motor pool could not get to start or run. One day the captain said he was going to Quarter Master to get a different jeep. They didn't have one for him, but while he was gone, only my third day there, I took an open end and box end wrench and readjusted the tappet setting on the valves of the engine and the motor started right up. Luckily, I had seen this done back home on the farm. When he came back and saw his jeep running, he was one happy captain. The next week I was promoted to the truck shop and received my first rank promotion to Private 1st Class, my first stripe on my sleeve.

This was the beginning of new promotions in my army hitch. Our company commander, a captain, began to use me for other details. He had me go along on three-day trips for company and mechanical support if needed. Also our battalion commander, a major, owned a big old Mercedes Benz passenger car. He would leave camp for the weekend and most times his Mercedes would quit running before he got back. We would take a truck and pull his Mercedes in to a local German garage mechanic. Then he would send me to talk German with the mechanic and try to explain what was wrong with the car. The major would give me candy and cigarettes to give the Germans as tips for favors. I got along well with my commanders and life was pretty easy.

Strive for excellence, not perfection.

Think big thoughts but relish small pleasures.

Watch a sunrise at least once a year.

Never waste an opportunity to tell someone you love them.
Have a firm handshake.
Don't expect life to be fair.
Life's Little Instructions

I took the position of a sergeant as soon as I had fixed that jeep for my captain. In the army you couldn't get promoted more often than once a month. I came into the motor pool as a private. Every month for five months straight, the army captain put another stripe on my sleeve until I had five stripes, not too bad for a dumb farm boy. By this time they were working hard on me to re-enlist for another three years. They offered to send me to commission officers training. While all this was going on my mother was praying I'd come home. Dad would write letters telling me to come home and help him farm. He also wrote my Captain and told him I was going home. He also offered me help to get my own farm going.

MIRACLE 8 The social part of army life was the toughest to put up with. Peer pressure was great. In Germany we stayed in big old houses, several guys in one room on single bunk army beds. I didn't like going out at night with the guys. Most all of them got drunk every night. I went to some shows and circus events with guys but stayed in most of the time. We all had pistols or revolvers in our footlockers. These were guns we bought off German people who needed money to live on. The guys were all good to me when they were sober. One night Tucker came home half drunk and got mad because I didn't go out with the guys. I was lying in bed. He took his pistol out of the footlocker and came over to me. He asked "Are you better than the rest of us?" holding the loaded pistol over my head, swearing at me and saying if I moved one inch he was going to shoot me! This lasted for 15 to 20 minutes,(seemed like an hour). I could easily have come home in a coffin. His gun was loaded and I knew it. My mother must have been home praying. I didn't move, I hardly breathed. One of the other guys came and got him away from me.

"My son, listen and accept my words and they will
multiply the years of your life. I have taught you
the way of wisdom, I have guided you along decent paths"
(Proverbs 4:10).

MIRACLE 9 Hitler had taken all the morality out of the German girls. They were taught to be used and abused by men any way a man wanted to do. There were always German girls hanging around our rooms. One girl, I don't even remember her name, got into bed with me four nights in a row. Mom must have really been praying. I can truthfully say that I never touched her. The guys would ask each morning, "Did you make out?" She gave up on me and moved in with another guy. Later, he went to the clinic and discovered he had VD (venereal disease). Most of those girls were carrying diseases.

One night I was in bed. Beds were close together and a girl was in bed with another man next to mine. After that man went to sleep the girl reached in my bed and attempted to focus on my private parts. I got out of there and never saw her again. PTL! I always thought she liked me better than the guy she was with. This girl too, gave my comrade VD.

"My son give me your heart; let your eyes find
happiness in my ways. A prostitute is a deep pit.
A loose woman is a narrow wall. She is like a
robber, lying in ambush. She spreads unfaithfulness
throughout society" (Proverbs 23:26-28).

As I mentioned before, World War II ended in August 1945 when Japan surrendered to the United States. An interesting point that has always stayed in my mind was that my best army buddy, Marvin, was with me all through basic training and even went overseas on the same boat. We were separated at LaHarve, France. Marvin went to Berlin, Germany and I was shipped to Austria. I thought I might never see my buddy Marvin again, but don't you know, coming back in September 1946, here was Marvin on the same ship I was on. Needless to say, we have kept in touch with each other, have vacationed together, and have always had good times together.

Jon and Marvin Clarkson
Army Buddies

The boat ride coming back from Europe was different than going over. No more big high bunk beds in the bottom of the boat and none of that seasick stuff. Because of the Army promotions up to Tec/Sgt (five stripes) I was offered a private room on the ship coming back. It was a small room but nice. Our meals were better. I ate with the commissioned officers. In this private room I had time to read and think of where my life was going. If I had any touch of salvation in Christ, I know I had lost it all by this time. The army life had gotten the best of me. I was miserable inside and did not want to go home that way. I did not want to disappoint my mother who had prayed for me every day I was gone.

He paid a debt He did not owe
I owed a debt I could not pay,
I needed someone
To wash my sins away.

GREATEST MIRACLE OF ALL I made an altar by my bedside, knelt and gave my heart to Jesus. This was a new life experience. I came away from this altar, washed by tears of repentance. I felt so clean and new. I just knew life had a new feeling. Everything looked brighter and the load of guilt was gone. I had a new friend in Jesus. I can't explain it fully, but it is wonderful. If you haven't tried it, you are missing the best part of life. You really need to try it, you can talk to Jesus just like another real person.

And now I sing a brand new song
Amazing grace;
Christ Jesus paid the debt
That I could never pay.

The first thing I did was clean up my duffel bag. A friend had given me part of a bottle of liquor. I never drank any of it. Don't really know why I kept it so long. Also had a carton of cigarettes that I had gotten through trading with other soldiers that needed money for their gambling. I never smoked any of that carton either. I'll never forget the day I walked to the edge of that ship, looked at the big blue ocean, waves fifty feet high, and threw them both overboard. It was ironic to have sins forgiven crossing the Atlantic Ocean. I found the Lord at sea level, 0 degrees altitude. Like the song goes, "my sins are buried in deepest sea, my sins are blotted out I know."

"You will tread our sins underfoot,
and hurl all our iniquities into the
depths of the sea" (Micah 7:19).

This confession took away all desires for either drinking or smoking. It was part of the clean-up from my altar experience. I am convinced every person needs his or her own private altar experience. You need to get down on your knees and talk to Jesus like you would talk to your best friend. Jesus is a real person and you will know when you have gotten his attention.

"Blessed is the one who is always
fearful of sin. But whoever is hard-
hearted falls into disaster" (Proverbs 28:14).

I have sat with many professional people in large conventions and political rallies where liquor was free, but it has never tempted me in the least. In my army life I saw what alcohol could do to people. There are many guys I've seen beaten up in fights all because they drank too much, got too loud for their own good, or had their noses broken because they got kicked in the face. I've seen it all.

"Wine makes people mock, liquor makes
them noisy, and everyone under their

influence is unwise" (Proverbs 20:1).
Oh! What a Savior, Oh! Hallelujah.
He gave his life blood for even me.

Marvin P. Dalton

I got back from overseas late in the fall of 1946, and I received an honorable discharge from the army in December 1946. During the winter of 46-47 I went to Indiana to look for work. I lived with my brother Adam and his wife Marcella. It was a fun winter. I landed a job at a furniture factory in Berne, Indiana where Adams where living. My job was everything from stacking wood to running planer sanders and some mill work. The winter went fast. I dated a girl for about two months. Betty was a real nice girl. Her dad had money and I almost stayed in Indiana. Adam said, I had just thrown a meal ticket out the window when I left Indiana.

⇒ *Four* ⇐
BACK TO THE FARM

In the spring of 1947 I went back to Brinsmade to work on the farm for Dad and Mom. The summer of 47 I turned 21. Dad said I could farm on my own the next year, 1948. I made plans to do that. I had some G.I. money coming to go to school, so decided to take one more year of high school at Leeds, North Dakota. This was the fall, winter and spring of 47-48. I really enjoyed high school bookkeeping and also took physics and took a typing class. I got straight A's, although I don't know how I did it. That winter I stayed with Uncle Mike and Aunt Martha O'Connell. Uncle Mike was a school bus driver so I rode on his bus to Leeds High School each day. One day Mr. Iverson, the school superintendent, asked me if I would drive Mike's bus. It worked out real well as I was going there everyday. Mike and Martha made a good home for me till spring when Mom and Dad got back from Florida. I then moved back with them.

Become the most positive and enthusiastic person you know.
Ask for a raise when you feel you have earned it.
Return a borrowed vehicle with the gas tank full.
Buy whatever kids are selling in their front yard.
Feed a stranger's expired parking meter.
Say "thank you" a lot, say "please" a lot.
Leave the toilet seat in the down position.
Put your tissue into the trash.
Life's Little Instructions

At this time in my life I began observing two young farmers in our neighborhood. Jim and Joe were cousins to each other. Jim took over his dads well established farm. I remember him driving by our Dads farm many times, to check on hired help he had in his farming operation, which included the farm right south of ours that Dad had to give up in the dirty thirties. Jim also had a custom harvesting operation and an airplane to fly to Kansas and Oklahoma to check on his harvest operation. Jim bought new cars, trucks, and equipment all of the best. An interesting note here was the fact that Jim also farmed the bottom land of Devils Lake, where he grew flax several years. Now Devils Lake is the largest lake in North Dakota and probably in the entire Northwest. Jim also was a popular figure in civic and political circles.

Joe came from a poor family home, his dad was an alcoholic. Joe started farming by renting 80 acres of ground. He rented used small equipment and worked hard, doing his own work, to get started.

I kept thinking, if I could only find myself somewhere in between Jim and Joe, thinking I would probably never own a combine, and for sure not an airplane, but I started and as time went on you will see.

Nineteen forty-eight was to be my first year of farming. Dad gave me 480 acres to farm. Dad sold me one of his tractors, a D-Case, and let me use his equipment to get started. In turn, I did seeding and work for him. This Case tractor was different than today. No cab, no heater and no air. The tractor was known as a plow tractor. That meant the tractor would follow a furrow made by the plow. We would be plowing late in the fall, sometimes we even plowed down fresh snow. Then it was cold on the tractor and we would get off and run to keep warm or we would run and catch baby rabbits. Sometimes we picked up stones to throw at birds or gophers. We did all these things while the tractor and plow were moving down the field.

Tabernacle at Lakewood Park Camp - 47-48

My first new automobile
1948 Ford Sedan cost $1800.00

This was the time period that Dad was helping build the new tabernacle at Lakewood Park Bible Camp. This project started in 1947 and ended in 1948 so it was good to help Dad on the farm for those two years. Dad was the main foreman on this 60 by 140 building. He must have been a good builder because 55 years later the building is still straight and is used every year. Dad was always building something, either at the farm or for someone else. He built the house, garage, barn, chicken coop, grain elevator and other buildings on our farm.

I went to the bank,

where Dad and Ezra banked, to borrow money for farming. The banker, Vic Helberg, asked what I had for collateral and "I said, nothing." He said, "on the performance of your dad and brother, Ezra," he would loan me enough to buy seed and fertilizer and some spray. Ezra was established in farming by this time and he helped me too. So with $3,000 borrowed money and no equity I was able to seed my first crop of wheat.

By this time I knew I needed help from a better source if I was going to succeed. One Sunday afternoon in June of 1948 I took a walk out behind the barn and down a path to one of my fields. I prayed all the way out and back asking the Lord for his help and guidance. In return I vowed to give to churches 10% and another 10% to missions of any profits I made. This was not an ordinary walk. I felt a real closeness to Jesus and a lifted spirit because I knew I had made an agreement with God. I have never forgotten that special day.

"Trust in the Lord with all your heart,
do not rely on your own understanding.
In all your ways acknowledge him, and
he will make your path smooth" (Proverbs 3:5-6).

When harvest time came that year, Dad, who was a custom thresher, harvested my crop. The crop was good that year. We had rain enough to produce a twenty bushel wheat crop, wheat was three dollars a bushel, the same price as it is today, but our costs were only 10 percent of what they are now. It gave me a good start for another year. Uncle Mike gave me his land to farm in 1949 so then I had 640 acres to farm.

The year 1949 offered a new experience. Ezra and I bought a used self-propelled combine and a used International truck. We loaded the combine on the truck and went to Kansas to harvest

Thousands of geese would fly over us as we worked in the field with our tractors.

Our first coop used combine and used 1946 INT Truck loaded for Kansas 1949. First service truck was a two wheel trailer.

wheat. We did this in 1949-50. In 1951 Dad bought a combine and went with us to Kansas. Prior to this time dad thought everything had to be put in bundles and threshed. It was hard for him to give up a system that had worked, probably since the beginning of time. When he saw how easy it was for us boys to harvest, it didn't take long for him to change systems. I can remember just before harvest in 1950 I had been looking at a new system of putting grain into the farm bin. Up to this point everything was shoveled off by hand with a scoop shovel. Larson Implement was introducing a new grain auger where you just dumped the grain out of the back of the truck and the auger took it into the bin. If you had a hoist on the truck you could lift that and the grain would flow into the auger. One day I came home with hoist on my truck and a grain auger behind. My Dad said, "Jonathan, don't buy everything you see up town, your going to go broke".

In 1950 Dad bought the John Deere business in Leeds. Dad had traded one of his farms to Mr. Hobson when buying the business in Leeds. Then in 1951 I got to farm the Hobson land, giving me another 480 acres to farm.

MIRACLE 11 One interesting side note during 1949-1950, I had been dating Delores Herman. It seems as though I won her parents more than Delores. We never really did hit if off too good. Her parents thought I was okay. Mr. George Herman offered to sell me one of his farms. This was the first chance I had to buy real estate, and what a deal he gave me! I didn't have to pay anything down and only paid 4% interest, and no real due date. You can see I didn't get the daughter but instead I got the farm. My first financial miracle in the farming venture. Uncle Mike said I missed out on a lifelong meal ticket. Second time I left a lifelong meal ticket go. Both our family and the Herman family had a lot in common. We were all farmers. There were five girls in the Herman family and six boys in ours. Most all of us boys dated a Herman girl at sometime during our school years. We probably were too much like rivals and that caused none of us to marry. The opportunity was sure there. Mr. Herman was considered one of the wealthiest men of his day. Another opportunity to marry money went out the window. I guess I just have to work for it.

George was also a hunter. I was in my twenties when he organized some field fox drives. His plan was to put at least 28 men around a 640 acre section of land, posting seven men on each side of the section. As they walked toward the center the men all came closer together surrounding the fox or rabbits within a close shooting range. It really worked well. Mr. Herman was as fair a shooter and honest as you could find. He was a great Christian example to me. He would put 20 dollars in the church offering when others threw in one dollar, 20 dollars would keep the pastor all week. 1 dollar bought 5 gallons of gas.

In 1950-1951 I started making trips to Tokio, North Dakota, as there was a little white Swedish girl that lived near the Indian Reservation. We went together that summer and at Christmas time in 1950 we were engaged. I was invited to spend Christmas Eve at Cleo's, parents house. The dinner was good and I said I liked the lutefisk, but I think I lied that part. Later it didn't seem to work out and we broke up in the spring of 1951. I must say Cleo was a nice girl. Cleo's brother, Ralph, was a good friend of mine. That winter of 1950-1951, I drove to Florida to see Mom and Dad. Ralph was teaching school nearby and he fed and watered my cattle.

MIRACLE 12 Having started farming and raising cattle, the Minnewauken School System conducted Ag-shop classes for farmers who wanted to learn welding or build small tools, etc.

While I was feeding baled hay, I thought I should make a bale hook. This was a hand held hook to pick up 50 lb. bales and place them out for cattle to feed on. The hook was all completed except to grind off the rough edges. As I was grinding, the hook caught on the grind wheel. It threw the hook right at my head, cutting off the top of my ear, went through my skull, and gave me a fractured skull. I was knocked out and down on the floor. A schoolmate and friend of mine, Don Herman, was there and picked me up, put me in his new Chevrolet car and hauled me to Devils Lake Hospital. Was I ever surprised to wake up in that place. Lying there five days, thinking and praying, a white figure came and stood at the end of my bed. It was either my guardian angel or Jesus. I prefer to think it was the latter. A healing took place and I had no bad effects from the accident. P.T.L.

Now back to farming, looking back at my walk "Out Behind The Barn," my salvation experience in the ship and the accelerated start in farming, it showed me the Lord had good things in store for me.

"Trust in the Lord with all thine heart and
lean not on thine own understanding.
In all thy ways acknowledge Him and He shall
direct thy path" (Proverbs 3:5-6).

In the years 1948-1952, being a single man and having the same farming interests as Ezra, I spent lots of time with him and Marguerite. I stayed at their house one winter out on the farm, six miles from town and another winter in Brinsmade, when they owned the big Herman house.

I remember the winter out at the farm. It was a cold winter with lots of snow and Ezra and I both left our cars, mine a new 1948 Ford, out on the road so they wouldn't get blocked in. The bad part was that at 20 degrees below zero, the cars wouldn't start if left out more than five hours, as they got so stiff they wouldn't crank. So, at 2 o'clock every night I would get out of bed, completely dress with a big overcoat, high overshoes, cap over my ears, flashlight in hand, in heavy mittens, and go out and start the cars. I'd sit out there about half an hour till the cars got good and warm, then shut them off, go back to the house, undress and go to bed. Sleep in? NO! By 9:00 o'clock the cars were stiff again. This didn't last all winter, thank the Lord. I got to go to Florida with Dad and Mom to break up the winter.

 The winter I lived in town with Ezra and Marguerite, we didn't have so much car trouble, although I remember some nights we left the cars idle all night. It took about five gallons of gas. Gas was only 20-30 cents a gallon so the cost was not too great. That winter Ezra and Marguerite wanted new kitchen cupboards. I bought an electric power table saw and Ezra and I built the cupboards. We had fun too.

 One night the three of us, roads all blocked with snow, temperature below zero, walked to our friends house, Don and Ruth Herman, two miles out in the country. We were treated to coffee and cake and at midnight walked back to town. The moon was full and was shining on the snow which gave light, about one half daylight. It was light enough to see rabbits and fox run over the road and in the field. With temperatures below zero things were crisp. The old fashioned telephone lines that stretched through the air about twenty feet above ground would hum you a tune that I can still hear in my memory today.

 During the early 50s Ezra and I tried beef cattle ventures and cow calf operations. We bought bred heifers from Montana. Ezra had an International truck that we took to Jordan, Montana, which proved to be long cold rides. There weren't good heaters in the trucks in the early 50s. Calving out these cows in snow and cold was something not easily forgotten. During the time cows were calving, I would check on them every four hours, 24\7. That meant dressing twice each night with heavy boots and clothing, go out in the cold with a flashlight in hand and move the new calf and cow into warm dry places. Occasionally the new calf would get cold and stiff, then we would bring the calf into the house to warm up. Laying him on an old carpet, I would fall asleep. When the calf warmed up he would try to stand up, only to find the kitchen linoleum was to slippery to walk on, as a new born baby trying to stand, what a noise he would make in the house, knock over the waist basket or the garbage can.

We had a big blizzard. It filled my cattle yard with three to five feet of snow. I got my neighbor Wayne Gerig to come with his caterpillar and push out the snow. As the snow was pushed up against the fences the snow got hard and so the cows could walk right out over the fence, causing one more problem.

MIRACLE 13 One summer day there was one bad episode. Ezra was out in a pasture fixing fence where he had cows and a bull. I just happened to stop by when I saw the bull chasing him. I put the truck in high gear and set out to help. Just in time, I got the truck between him and the bull and pushed the bull over the fence. Nobody knows what could have happened had I not been there.

"The name of the Lord is a strong tower A righteous
person runs to it and is safe" (Proverbs 18:10).

By this time farming seemed to be my nitch. I was renting more land and bought a second half section, was doing more combining and in the year 1951 I also helped Dad run the Ford business in

Leeds. I didn't care much for that type of business. Seemed people were hard to satisfy. Retailers, you have my sympathy.

The early fifties was a time of turning point, before I got married, when a change had to be made. Shep had gotten older, had been with me through my teens and up until I started making more long trips to Kulm to see Fern. Shep, a friend to the whole family, had been left a day or two at a time on his own. My three younger brothers were gone, some to a collage, or maybe south for the winter with Mom and Dad. I was no longer feeding cattle or around to care and feed Shep. When I would see him, he looked so lonely. I don't remember ever telling my siblings that I finally laid him to rest. Shep left many memories and a hollow spot on the farm.

Five
ROMANCE

My younger brother Paul had already gotten married to Jean Carlson from Kulm, North Dakota. Paul was an ordained minister, and had been a pastor at Walhalla, North Dakota. Paul and Jean were just starting in the ministry, doing pastoral work and evangelism. They needed another person with musical ability for support. They picked a pretty young lady from Kulm for this position. This made them a well sounding trio. As they traveled around from city to city, many times their route brought them through Brinsmade, stopping at the farm of Dad and Mom. I got well acquainted with this pretty Kulm girl. She was a good singer and could she ever play the piano! I remember her coming to Dad and Mom's house before I ever went to the Army. She was quite young then and pretty. I had no idea she would still be around when I got back home from service in the Army.

One weekend in the summer of 1952, Silas and I decided to go to Kulm to look over the crop (girls that is). We both took a girl for a ride in the country. Silas never went back. I went back a month later to go to church on Sunday night. After church I asked that pretty girl if she needed a ride home. She said, "Give me a few minutes and I'll be back." I didn't know at the time she had come to church with another guy and he was to take her home again. But, she came back and said, "Yes, let's go." I stole her away right out of church. Now this pretty girl was Fern Johnson who lived in Swede township. Swede township was exactly just that. People were very proud to be Swedish. For a German like me to get in was something you tried at night. Going there was a task in the wintertime. The roads would block with snow and in the springtime roads would go under water. But, I persisted to go in and get that Swede. Amazingly, the second time I went out to pick up Fern at the farm we were riding to Kulm and on my second glance at her while driving I knew she was the one I wanted to marry, maybe it was the way the sun shone through the car windshield, I don't know but my heart flipped. It's that initial feeling that only comes once. My heart throbbed, I wondered how long will it be.

We dated the rest of 1952 and after Christmas I asked if she would marry me. Dating a girl 150 miles from home took some sleepless nights.

Fern was definitely a church going girl with high moral values. She was very involved in church choir and music. She sang in trios and was a good piano player. It didn't take long to learn that Fern was the best of cooks. Fern was working for Evert and Elwood, two of her brothers, at their farm during our time of courtship. Fern was so loyal to those guys. When I would come to pick her up she would ask me if

Fern - about the time we started dating

she had time to wash the kitchen floor or put away the dishes or take the homemade bread out of the oven before we went out. Man, homemade bread, I could just stay there and start eating. Now I appreciate that aspect of her more than ever. Nothing is ever left undone, if it takes all night to do it. She is sweet!

Never underestimate the power of love.
Compliment even small improvements.
Keep your promises, no matter what.
Don't be afraid to say, "I made a mistake."
Don't be afraid to say, "I don't know."
Marry only for love.
Call your Mother.

Life's Little Instructions

We kept in contact by phone and mail, and after New Year's the call came through. She said, "The answer is yes." I knew what she meant but she sounded so bashful about it. I said, "You mean yes," and she replied, "Yes, I'll marry you." Whoa! Was I happy! We got engaged on Valentine's Day 1953 and went to her sister Marilyn's and her husband Paul Gage for Sunday dinner to celebrate. We had a great courtship! I would go down to her farm home on Saturday evening, and we would go around town and other places. Kulm didn't have much for hotels so finding a place to stay overnight was a problem. A few different week-ends Pastor Jorgenson invited me to stay with him. We had some good talks. One statement he made was, "Fern is so graceful." It just took away all doubts, I knew I had the right girl for me. Sunday we went to church morning and evening. For lunch we went to cafes or sometimes to friends of hers like Frank's or Carl Carlson's home or Fern's brother, Stanley and his wife, Helen, would invite us. I would get her back to the farmhouse by midnight, kiss her goodbye and start the 150-mile trip back to Brinsmade. Sometimes I stopped to sleep halfway home. I usually stopped to eat in Jamestown to wake up. Some nights I got home in the morning in time to dress for work.

One weekend in April, Fern came home with me to Dad and Mom's house. That next week we had our blood tests taken and got our marriage license. This same weekend Martha Peltz had come home with Silas. They were also engaged. This was a time to make plans for weddings. We wanted them close together so friends could take in both weddings on the same trip. The four of us rode around together in the car and talked about plans for dates and some talk about our honeymoons. Silas and Martha wanted a June 7th wedding at Glen Ullen, North Dakota, and we chose a date as close as we dared which was June 9th at Kulm. There wasn't much time for travel when the two cities were 200 miles apart.

MIRACLE 14 Planning for the wedding was done in a hurry. Fern's mom had passed away when Fern was only nine years of age and her dad passed away when she was 16. Fern was keeping house for her two bachelor brothers at the home farm when we were planning our wedding. The brothers were not excited about her getting married because that meant they would lose their housekeeper. So she planned and paid for the wedding without their help. Money was tight. She chose a beautiful white bridal gown, but the attendants wore pastel colored gowns, worn at her sisters wedding two years before. Most of the flowers were lilacs that we picked from the bushes in Fredonia. The lilac bushes at home were done bearing so we were glad to find some in Fredonia. We were married in the Assembly of God church in Kulm, North Dakota where Lloyd Jorgenson was pastor. Lloyd was such a great help in planning the wedding. He had ideas that we never would have thought of.

Her attendants were her sister, Lillet, Marjorie Loven, a very close friend and Elaine Loven, the flower girl. I chose for my attendants my brother, Paul, and Morris Sjostrom, Fern's brother-in-law and the ring bearer was my nephew, Wayne Liechty. Rev. Lloyd Jorgenson, Fern's pastor and mentor and of course a good friend of mine, officiated. Jean Liechty was organist and my brother, Silas, who got married two days before us, was the soloist. Silas and Martha stayed back for our wedding before leaving on their honeymoon. Our wedding was not so fancy but it was special to us. The reception was held in the church fellowship hall and so many friends came.

After the reception and gifts were opened and the church put back in order, we went to look for our car. Somebody, I know who they were, had taken my car to another garage, blocked up the back wheels and left the air out of the tires. As luck would have it, Morris Sjostrom, one of my attendants and now my new brother-in-law, was a mechanic at the Ford garage. He got an air compressor and helped us get going.

We got as far as Jamestown the first night and rolled into bed at 2:30 A.M. This was our first night in the same bed. We left for our honeymoon about noon the next day. Heading for Yellowstone National Park, the whole world looked different. I wasn't alone anymore.

We spent several days around Yellowstone. It was fun to watch the geysers spout up and see the hot water pots. We also took a couple of tours. Several nights, there were bears rattling the garbage cans and snorting at our door, the sounds woke us. These night sounds just made Fern come a little closer. It was a great

Our wedding picture June 9, 1953

surprise to meet Silas and Martha at the same place. Strange, we couldn't even honeymoon apart. We talked about all four of us sleeping in the same room. It could save a little cash! On second thought we decided to spend the money. We had a couple picnics together and met each other at some sight seeing areas. We finally found our way back to North Dakota. I knew I had found my prize.

"Who can find a wife with strong character?
She is worth far more than jewels. Her husband
trusts her with all his heart, and he does not lack
any good thing. She helps him all the days of her life"
(Proverbs 31:10-12).

At this point, Fern was 100% with my ideas and desires, no doubt about it. The main thrust here was to fix up the farmhouse that came with the farm George Herman sold to me. Fern knew what the house looked like before we got married. We had looked at it and I asked her if she would move in the old house with me. Her response I'll never forget. She said, "I would move into the old garage behind the house, with no door left on it, one wall caved in and roof sagging, if it was with you." WOW! The house wasn't modern, no bathroom and no running water. We went in and cleaned up and painted the entire inside. We lived at my mom and dad's farm the first three months and looked for furniture for the old house. Fern had lived with her brothers at the Kulm farm cooking and keeping house for them so she had no furniture and I had always lived with my folks so I didn't have any either. We were both eager to get into our own place no matter what! We found a used bed, one old kitchen type cupboard, a few old chairs and moved in. I remember our first table was put together with apple boxes and a piece of plywood, but we didn't suffer. Fern started right in, cooking full course meals and cleaning the house as if it was a new house. She knew how to wash walls and scrub floors and wash clothes. It was always a treat to come home from work. Her older brothers Evert and Elwood had brought her up right.

In one of our conversations about farming, and she knew she was marrying a farmer, I asked her if she would milk cows with me. Fern had practiced milking for her dad and brothers. Fern in her super natural wisdom responded, "I'll milk as many as you do." As luck would have it, I didn't want to milk cows so neither of us ever milked. Guess we both milked cows enough for our parents. She is still applying this wisdom on me today.

We were plenty busy getting the crops in, as this was harvest time. Silas and Martha were living at Mom and Dad's too, right after marriage. All four of us worked in the harvest. Fern and Martha were truck drivers, while Silas and I ran the combines. Silas had some interest in farming as he and I had purchased the Adrian Buttz Quarter. Little did we know what that would lead to.

After harvest of 1953, Fern and I took our farm truck and went to Fargo to look for household furniture. It was time to throw out the apple boxes. We came back with a new stove, refrigerator, kitchen table and chairs, bedroom set, sofa and chair. A kitchen sink and cabinets were also purchased. The old house began to look more like home. The house did not have a bathroom or toilet so we rigged up a homemade pot for the first winter. The next summer we put in running water and a bathroom. Water was pumped from the cistern under the house. We bought water to keep the house going. Fern always had plenty of coffee and food to go with her good baking. I did luck out the second year of marriage, Fern could not remember if my birthday was in June or July, that

year I got two cakes. Like one guy said:
"His wife would never talk in the morning
till she got some coffee in her."
He said, "The best thing he could do
Was to hide the coffee pot."
But not really, Fern is not a nonsense talker,
but rather a woman of wisdom.

Harvest scenes in Kansas

⇉ *Six* ⇇
BUILDING A BUSINESS

The years 1953-1956 rolled along fast. We got into a pattern where I was farming and helping some at Dad's John Deere and Ford business and Fern was doing bookkeeping for Dad at the stores. Farming was growing and I continued the southern harvest combining. Dad and Mom went combining three years and they took Frank Harris along. He talked a lot and would get up on his knees in bed and wave his hands and argue. It was always an interesting sight. Fern and I also chose help like Earl Loken, Wayne Rolle, Darwin Verke and others. We had a travel trailer along where Fern and the children could spend time during the days and make noon and early evening lunches. The men stayed in motels. Fern was great at cooking and making lunches as we traveled from one job to another. Fern didn't really like it, especially the severe thunderstorms in Kansas. The thunder was so loud it really shook that little camper we had. Fern would grab me and ask, "Are we okay, Jon?"

Back at home, Silas was working for Dad at the John Deere store and trying to find his place in life. Silas and Martha had an invitation to go to Jamestown as associate pastor in 1955. I thought this was the end of our farming and business as partners. One thing we claimed early in our business life was the 1st Psalm:

> "Blessed is the man who does not walk in the counsel
> of the wicked or stand in the way of sinners or sit in the
> seat of mockers. But his delight is in the law of the
> Lord, and on his law he meditates day and night. He is
> like a tree planted by the water, which yields its fruit in
> season and whose leaf does not wither. Whatever he

does prospers. Not so the wicked! They are like chaff that wind blows away. Therefore the wicked will not stand in judgment, nor sinners in the assembly of the righteous for the Lord watches over the way of the righteous, but the way of the wicked will perish"
(Psalm 1:1-6).

By this time Fern had decided to earn some cash of her own. She took an office job working for Ezra who was running Dad's John Deere store. Nineteen fifty-five was a good year for farming. Fern needed a better car to drive to work, so we bought a new 1956 two-door hard top Fairlane Ford. What else could we buy when Dad was selling Fords? This was good for Fern. She got out of the house more and felt more needed. Ezra began working for Dad at John Deere and I took over some of his farming.

Our church connections at this time were something else. It was in our first or second year of marriage, Gerald and Beulah Derstine came to Leeds with a Gospel Revival tent. Amos and Joy Stoltsfus were along with Derstine as song leader. Our Dad had met them in Florida. After the tent meetings we helped start a Revival Center on Main Street. The Hoffs, the Groffs and the Liechtys were the start up which was hard work. We lived one and a half miles from Brinsmade where there was a good Christian and Missionary Alliance Church. We went there part of the time and attended some of the social events. Dad and Mom had gone to Minnewauken to the Union Gospel Tabernacle and wanted us to help there. They needed Fern as their piano player, and I helped in Sunday school. Really we were going three places. Dad was on the church board along with Erick Silberg and Frank Harris. It seemed they didn't get enough of each other at church, so many Sundays they all came to Mom's for Sunday noon dinner. That was the type of hodgepodge I grew up in. This was real disturbing to Fern. We never knew where we were going from one Sunday to the next.

The only church that was like the one Fern grew up in was the Assembly of God Church in Devils Lake. This was 30 miles from home. It kind of worked out that we floated around to the local three in the mornings and went to church at Devils Lake most Sunday nights.

Mom's Sunday dinners were really good. I'll never know how she did it. People from the Minnewauken Church would come out without notice. Mom had home canned cooked meat along with potatoes and a large garden of greens. She could get dinner for a big crowd in one hour's time. The garden was nearly an acre in size. All kinds of vegetables, melons, corn and even flowers were raised. We boys pulled a lot of weeds and hoed the garden. Sometimes we took a saltshaker to the garden, picked off a juicy ripe tomato, or pulled up a big fresh carrot and had a good feast right there.

In 1956 Silas and Martha drove up from Jamestown to visit us and have dinner. They also asked Fern and me to come to Jamestown to look at a farm that was for sale. I told Fern we could probably take off a day and go but was sure nothing would come of it. It so happened we stayed the second day and bought a nice 960-acre farm, jointly half and half with Si and Martha.

There was a renter on there for that year and in 1957 and in 1958 we were able to get Edwin and Luella Nitschke to move on the farm and help us. This farm was the headquarter site of an operation called "The Chicago Ranch". There was a big two-story house, three barns, and many small granaries, plus two silos. At one time they farmed 3,000 acres from this farm site, all with horses. In the late 40s this place was split up and sold to the farmers, one section, 640 acres, at a time.

About this time of year there were heavy talks of forming a partnership between three of us brothers. Nothing had been put on paper. No inventories or by-laws, we were only in the talking stage. Since we had purchased the farm south of Jamestown we did agree to work it.

In the summer of 1957 the three guys decided to make hay on our new farm by Jamestown. Fern and I went down to help. Needing a place to live we took a used mobile home and parked it three miles away from the farm on Judith and Wesley Loven's farm. Judith and Fern were sisters.

We were in there about a week when Silas came out and said he sold the mobile home. With nowhere to go we moved into Wesley's old car garage. No water, no toilet, no heat and no air. Fern cooked on a kerosene burner and we ate off our laps. We had a bed in there. The crickets were so bad we put coffee cans under all four legs of the bed and put kerosene in the cans to keep the crickets out of the bed. The spiders on the wall were fun to watch too. Lovens cat hung around and kept the mice out anyway. We hurried haying, finished in about two weeks and went back to the Brinsmade area to farm. As life would have it, we were determined we could farm both ends, North and South (120 miles a part), at the same time. This worked quite well for a few years. We were short of tractor power. We were lucky enough to have the first Model R John Deere diesel tractor that our Dad got in at his John Deere business at Leeds. This was a revolution in tractor power and we were the envy of other farmers. Now we used that tractor at both ends. We had nothing to haul it on and the tractor would only go 16 miles an hour at cruising speed, so we pulled it the 120 miles back and forth with a truck. It was a two-man operation with one man steering the tractor. Then we could go twice as fast.

We had another great event during this time. In the fall of 1957, Fern, after three miscarriages since our wedding date, became pregnant again. On May 31, 1958 we became parents of Sherry Lu. What a great bundle of joy! Sherry was born at the Rugby Hospital 40 miles away. It was a hard delivery. I felt so bad and there was nothing I could do to help. I remember Fern wanted me close by and yet when the pain was so bad, she didn't. We were really glad when Sherry arrived. We spent that summer in our little shack on the farm watching Sherry grow and make funny noises and cute faces. What a beautiful time of life. Sherry seemed to grow so fast. It was really good for Fern to be a new mother, the greatest calling for a woman. In October, we left our home of five years and moved to a basement apartment in Jamestown. These were stressful times, moving and still farming at both locations. I would leave early mornings, go back up north 100 miles to Brinsmade, stay a few days and leave Fern and Sherry at home. I always had a great welcome back. We both felt we were doing the Lord's will. Fern was able to get involved in a church of her kind, which was the Assembly of God Church on 8th street and 8th avenue. This was only half a block from our basement apartment. She felt at home there anyway. Leaning on my "out behind the barn" experience and still giving 20% to charities, it seemed we both claimed the promise of Deuteronomy. 8:18:

> "God is our source, but you shall remember
> the Lord your God for it is he who is giving
> you power to make wealth."

It was with this frame of mind that we pursued enlarging our operations to create more income with more profits to give to charities. We were led to many good connections, which helped make all this possible.

Fern by our church on 8th Ave and 8th St, Jamestown

The Liechty Boys
Seated left to right: Jonathan, Adam, Ezra
Standing left to right: Reuben, Paul, Silas

Seven
THE START OF SPECIAL CONNECTIONS

About this time Silas and I, with our wives, had formed a partnership, which included Ezra and Marguerite. Ez and Marguerite had already moved to Jamestown and were helping Silas at the office.

(For future reference I will refer to this partnership as JES, which stood for Jon, Ezra and Silas).

How could I be so fortunate as to get two smart brothers to let me join them? Looking back I can see times when they laughed at some of my decisions. I was using an old Ford pickup on the farm. The heater didn't work and one of the boys laughed at the fact that I thought it to be a problem. Again I laid out a plan I thought was saving us all money and one of the boys said, "You aren't saving anything." Another brother said to me, "I can't believe you do the things you do." One time they were making fun of me in front of a friend of mine and he asked, "What's wrong with Jon?" My friend thought I was okay. Some of it may have been in fun, the Lord knew I needed help when I took my walk "out behind the barn." Jesus gave me some good connections when He hooked me up with my brothers. After all, I am their brother and there is nothing they can do about that. You'll learn more about connections later in this book.

A little background of how we got started in the mobile homes business might be helpful. While Silas and Martha moved to Jamestown to work in the church, he also had to make a living. Having connections with Dad's franchise at Leeds, he could get a mobile home at factory cost. He bought one to live in. While living in it he advertised it for sale. The home sold quickly and they drove to the factory with their Mainline Ford car and got a second new home. Advertising it again, it sold quickly. Off to the factory for the third home. This was repeated five or six times. It was time to go into a full-time business selling mobile homes.

Silas opened a sales lot on the south side of town. This was the beginning of Liechty Homes. Mr. Rabel sold him enough land to start a sales lot and a mobile home park. To sell mobile homes you need a place to park them. We did some planning, bought several acres from Mr. Rabel and built Holiday Park Village.

Here was our chance to get out of that basement apartment. We ordered a new 10 ft. wide by 50 ft. long home. Thinking our timing was right, we could move into the new park. A delay in park construction had us parking our new home out in West Town. This was a poor spot. No grass, no sidewalks, gravel driveway and our garbage we dumped in an open pit in the ground. We moved into our Holiday Park Village late in the fall of 58. Holiday and Western Park Village were built in three different settings with a total of 370 lots.

The next summer went fast. I took a six-week hitch in the combining business. Fern stayed at Kulm at the home farm where her sister and brother-in-law, Vernette and Rolland Sjostrom were working for her brothers, Evert and Elwood Johnson. The highlight of this summer was waiting for the arrival of another child. Jeffrey Jon was born October 25, 1959.
This was an easier delivery, I was so thrilled and now I had my son. I wondered what next.

I remember that date for two reasons. The big thing of course was Jeffrey. The second was that we had ordered a new 1959 Ford car and that arrived while Fern was in the hospital so I brought home a new baby and a new car.

This was the age of Sherry and Jeffrey when we traveled to Florida with Mr. and Mrs. Riffe.

Now we had lots of excitement in our new mobile home with two little babies to play with and care for. I can remember each of their first birthdays, the pictures we took, and the cakes the children messed up as they ate with lots of frosting on their faces and down on the floor.

While living here, Fern found room for her Hammond Organ. It doesn't seem possible that we could make tapes for a radio broadcast here, but Rev. G. L. Riffe, then our pastor, would come to our home with a recorder and tape out a radio broadcast. We had lots of fun and activities in our new 10' wide by 50' long mobile home.

In 1958 the Brown Farm came up for sale. JES managed to put money down and bought 480 acres adjoining our 960. Up to this time I had been banking at Minnewaukan Bank where I first started. I kept increasing my operating loans each year until the loans exceeded the banking limits. Mr. Helberg said, "Jon you're exceeding our banking limits, but we will still go with you. You are one of our biggest customers." I was glad for the reputation our dad and Ezra had built for me. Now to start farming in the Jamestown area, I needed a banker to help me there. I went to 1st National Bank and got turned down flat. The banker asked how many cattle I was going to have on the farm and I responded with " NONE." The banker said this was a cattle farm and they were not interested.

MIRACLE 15 Some years later, we did have cattle on this farm. But in the meantime I walked across the street to Jamestown National Bank and was introduced to Fritz Buegel. Mr. Buegel had just moved to the Jamestown Bank recently from a Cando bank. Now Cando was right close to our Brinsmade and Leeds area. Although we had never banked at Cando, Fritz knew our name and reputation. He gave me all the money I needed without a budget and continued that way getting up to six digit figure loans, as long as he was in the bank. This was another good connection.

I believe the Lord had him move to Jamestown and be ready just for us. That walk "out behind the barn" was working. Praise the Lord.

In the fall of 1959, a farm came up for sale next to the Brown Farm. We really made a big blunder. I was harvesting the crop at Brinsmade. Ez and Si were working at sales in Jamestown. I knew the right thing to do was to buy that 520 acres. I was busy up there. I mailed a check down to Ez and Si and told them to tie up the farm till I got there. I couldn't believe it, when a few days later the check came back. Ez and Si thought we were moving too fast. I was really disappointed. Our neighbor Mr. Anderson bought it. Mr. Anderson was a good neighbor to work with. Now Mr. Anderson has passed on and that would really have tied in and made a good farm unit.

Our church and social life had begun in Jamestown. It was the closest town with real shopping. Little did we know how many trips it would take to town to make life possible and a little enjoyable. However, Montpelier had a good school system with bus service at our door. We thought the children would like the school and would have advantages in the smaller school. Living on the farm would have many advantages for me. I could go home for most meals and always try to be home for breakfast and devotions with Fern and the children. We could pray for protection for the children at school and for all the activities on the farm, for wisdom and guidance.

"The fear of the Lord is the beginning
of knowledge. Stubborn fools despise
wisdom and discipline" (Proverbs 1:7).

While we were trying to decide where to live, the Everding farm, 480 acres, came for sale. This was now the 3rd part of the old Chicago Ranch that JES bought on the south side of our headquarters.

We made the decision to move out to the farm and fix up the big old house. We put in water and a sewer, put in a new furnace, repainted the inside and out, and added more kitchen cupboards and once again felt like we were really living. We moved out there in the summer of 1961. Having gotten settled in the house on the farm I thought there must be mornings I could take an extra hour and sleep. Awaking, I might have prayed:

Dear God
So far today, I've done all right.

I haven't gossiped. I haven't.
I haven't lost my temper, I haven't
lied or cheated, I haven't been
greedy, grumpy, nasty, selfish or
over-indulgent. I am very
thankful for that. But, in a few
minutes, Lord, I'm going to get
out of bed, and from then on,
I'm going to need a lot more help. Amen.

This was also the year JES opened a sales lot for mobile homes in Bismarck. Marvin Eckman had been in training at the Jamestown office for two years. Marvin and Marjorie took the position there. It was great to have good honest reliable people in charge in Bismarck.

As we entered the 60s, the momentum really began to grow. In 1963 we began making plans to build a new house on the farm. Yes, we liked living out there well enough to build. We looked at plans and contacted builders and gave a contract in the fall of 1963 to Art Swanson.

That same winter we wanted to go to Florida to see Dad who had contracted cancer of the liver. We've always enjoyed traveling with other people. Rev. and Mrs. G. L. Riffe were our pastors and we got them to go along to Florida. We took our 1960 Olds and left for two weeks. We had a great time with the Riffes. Sherry and Jeffrey were 5 and 4 years old. Riffes liked our kids and the kids liked them. Lots of funny things happened on the trip. One was when G. L. was going to give Mrs. Riffe a ride on Dad's two-seated bicycle. They were riding along side of a shallow road ditch with water in it. G. L. lost his balance and both of the Riffes rolled into the water. The sun was bright and shining, their clothes dried off real soon. We ate plenty of oranges and strawberries and Mom Liechty's good cooking.

Brother Riffe bought us and the kids plenty of ice cream and candy. We stopped at Ruby Falls, Kentucky, and picked pecans in Georgia, enjoyed glass bottom boats at Ocala, Florida and other points of interest. We all returned home in two weeks. Dad did not look good at that time and I was glad I got to spend this time with him.

We farmed that year and in the fall JES bought 1120 acres of the Henry Erickson farm. By this time we had acquired Ezra's 960 acre farm into the JES partnership. Now it was a challenge to upgrade and expand equipment to farm 4000 acres.

We will never forget 1964, as this is the year our Dad passed away. After having built a new house in Pinecraft, Florida and partially moved into the house in March, Dad had surgery for cancer of the liver. He never got very well after this. In June the doctor said, "If you want to go to North Dakota, go now." Dad and Mom came to Jamestown and Dad went right to the hospital. He only lived one week. His funeral service was at the First Assembly of God Church in Jamestown. Burial was at the Brinsmade Cemetery, west of town. The grave was beside our sister, Ruth. Mom stayed on the farm at Brinsmade the rest of the summer. That fall she moved into a new 10X50 mobile home in Holiday Park Village. Silas arranged to set the house right adjacent to their home. That was great for Mom, she lived there 24 years. These were great years for many of her seventeen grand children living in the Jamestown area. She fixed many lunches and Sunday dinners for anyone that wanted to stop by.

We were in the new house construction mode trying to keep up with that and with the mobile home business uptown. By this time,

Gene Wolff started working for us in the summertime at age 16. Later, Gene married Shirley and was living on our Everding farm. In time their little daughter Jeania was born. Gene helped us year round and tended our cattle in the wintertime. A very dependable man, always on time.

Nineteen sixty-four was also the year the big Yellow Monster drove in our yard and hauled Sherry away for 1st grade at Montpelier school. That's when school life began for us. Little did we know what all the activities would be for the next twelve years, sports, music, home economics, class trips, etc.

The following summer we moved into our new house. Watching the children as we moved into the new house was fun. They had been up to the house enough times they knew which room was theirs. They each had a bedroom. Jeff and Sherry both marched right in as though they had done it many times. Jeff would be six years of age in October, so in September he started 1st grade in Montpelier. This was easier because Sherry was in the second

House covered with snow March 1966

grade already.

We were well settled in and enjoyed the winter sports of snow mobile riding until March of 1966 when a 3-day blizzard came upon us. We didn't go out of the house the last two days of the storm. We had 36 inches of snow with strong winds. The snow piled up very high, it made snow banks over the house, completely covering half of the house under the snow. We could walk on snow right over the house. There was enough snow to ride our snowmobiles over top of the house. We shoveled our way out of the house and into the farm shop to get a tractor out to open driveways and barns. We had no car garage. After the storm we couldn't find the car. I started digging down where I thought the car stood. Digging down 5 feet into the snow, I finally found the roof of our car. Clothes lines, garbage cans, and even the electric meter, were all covered up. It took two more days for roads to open up so the school bus could run and so we could get to town for mail and groceries.

We didn't know if we had any cattle left. They didn't get feed or water for three days. Fortunately, enough of the cattle survived in a huddle in the barn, but now we had to find feed for the cattle under all the snow.

Thou wilt keep him in perfect peace,
whose mind is stayed on thee:
because he trusteth in thee
(Isaiah 26:3).

April came, it warmed up, and the snow started to melt. Water ran all over the creek south of our house and flooded over. Finally it got dry enough so we could go farming again.

This same year, 1966, JES looked at plans to build Skyway Mobile Home Park in Bismarck. This would provide 400 spaces to sell and place homes in the capital city. Business was good in home sales, even if we didn't stay open for business on Sundays.

Remember the Sabbath day to keep it holy.

Six days shalt thou labor and do all thy work
(Exodus 20: 8-9).

MIRACLE 16 Next came Charles DeLair to sell us his farm. Let's go back to the beginning of this story. We had moved out to the farm back in 1961. The DeLair farm joined our farm on the south side. Each winter, northwest winds blew snow off our farm filling his yard with big piles of snow. We had been over there a few times for coffee. It was a pain to see him move all that snow out after every storm. One day we offered him to plant trees on our farm for a windbreak to stop this snow. He asked "Would you really let me do that?" We said, "Yes, go ahead and there's no charge for the ground." He planted about two acres of ground to trees. We were so surprised that only two years later Chuck DeLair offered to sell us his farm. He didn't advertise at all. He said he wanted us to have the farm. JES made the down payment and bought another 720 acres of the Old Chicago Ranch.

After the sale, Chuck and Rita DeLair moved to Oregon. We remained friends, visiting them out west twice and they back here. Another DeLair family, Hank and Ruby, were close neighbors. Their children rode the school bus along with our children. When Hank decided to quit farming, back in the 70s, he asked a nephew, Frances Lee, to farm their 1000 acres of ground. These families have been great friends. We had the privilege of praying with Hank before he passed away. It is amazing how long friendships can last.

MIRACLE 17 After their nephew quite, we began farming the 1000 acre tract for Hank and Ruby back in the 80s, have farmed there place ever since and have a new contract this year for 2007.

We thank the Lord for blessing our cup of cold water to Mr. DeLair. We tried to be faithful in doing our part for the Lord. By now we were able to give 30% of our income to charity. We still took time to shut the farm down on Wednesday nights for Bible studies and took the children to church.

"The Lord is my Shepherd. I shall not want. He makes me lie down in green pastures. He leads me beside still waters. He restores my soul. He leads me in the paths of righteousness for His namesake. Even though I walk through the valley of the shadow of death, I will fear no evil, for you are with me. Your rod and staff, they comfort me"

(Psalm 23:1-4).

⇒ *Eight* ⇐
EXPANDING REAL ESTATE

If you remember earlier in the book I was watching Jim and Joe. Now I found two more model farmers I should observe. Bill and Ben where the two biggest farmers I knew, but wasn't always sure of their motives.

There were times in the late seventies and eighties when these two guys bought most all the farm real estate that came up for sale. They worked men and equipment as much as possible, they had no time for church on Sundays or Bible studies during the week. Seemed they could outbid anyone buying farm land. We bid against them one time, they blew us out of the water.

We went on a farm tour to Bills farm. They had a special barn for six of the biggest tractors you could buy and enough equipment to fill the whole farm yard.

Ben had 10 tractors, 10 planters, 10 cultivators and ten of each other thing he needed. Ben had airplanes, motor homes and fancy horse trailers. I thought they really knew something about farming that I didn't know. Seemed like nothing could ever stop Bill and Ben, I just kept watching.

In 1967, JES bought the 525 acre Mayer farm which laid on the banks of Beaver Creek. This farm had a good small house, barn and shop. One of our hired help and his family lived here. One spring beaver creek jammed up a big ice dam. When the ice let loose water flooded the entire valley where the house set. The water picked up the house off the foundation and floated it down to the bridge at the Montpelier road. There it stood still a little bit, started swirling round and round with the water and disappeared down under the bridge, that water swirl must have completely dismantled that house, never to be seen again. This has been an interesting farm for sportsmen. A small creek runs the entire length of the farm, has lots of trees and high hill slopes to hunt on. All of our families have hunted there. The farm has drawn hunters all the way from Minnesota and Texas. The focal point of our hunting seems to be there. Over one half of our deer have been taken on this farm. Yet many deer have escaped, dogging our spray of bullets.

The Mayer farm always produced a lot of deer and good hunting.

Silas, Ezra and I decided to take a real big hunting trip to Alaska. We loaded up all our hunting gear, clothing and some food supplies in a ¾ ton four-wheel-drive GMC truck and started driving to Skagway. The trip up was real successful. We took turns driving, never stopping to sleep. We each took turns trying to sleep in the back of the truck. It was my turn to sleep in the back when all of a sudden the pickup truck came to a screeching halt.

It was night time, we were on the Alaskan-Canadian highway where in the middle of the road, stood two big moose. The glare of the headlights made the moose look like monsters. That was the end of sleep that night. I crawled back into the truck, our blood literally boiling. We arrived at Gil and Mildred Meroney's house the third day. Now to get back up into the area to hunt, we could only go up on the river bottom. There were no established roads up there. Gil had loaded the trailer with lots of food and camping supplies which we hooked to a model H International tractor that Silas had hauled up to Alaska on a trailer on a previous trip. I must say we ate well up in the brush. We had baked ham, barbeque ribs, baked potatoes and all that good stuff. You knew this wasn't Gils first trip up the river to hunt by the way he laid in the supplies. Our plan was to hunt five days and return. On the third day it started raining, and filled up the river so we had no way of getting out of there. Our five-day hunt, turned into seven days, until the river went back down so we could travel. There were still deep water areas in the river we had to go through. One spot was so deep, the water completely covered the tractor motor and exhaust system. The tractor just plain died. With the four-wheel-drive GMC truck we pulled the tractor up on dry land. By now it was nighttime. The tractor was wet and the motor full of water. We began by draining out the oil, pulling out the spark plugs and taking off the magneto. It was cold and misting, we needed heat to dry our selves and the equipment. I don't know how Gil ever thought about bringing enough oil along to make a complete change. The other guys did all the work, but I, with my raynaud's (cold hand) disease, just couldn't get warmed up. By daylight, which comes early in the morning in Alaska, we were ready to continue our way back to Skagway. Oh! Yes we did get a young cow moose and a really large bull moose. The bull dressed out at nearly 800 pounds. We had our trophies hung up high enough in the trees so when the bear came in at night they couldn't get the meat. The bear did rattle our tie down chains a few times. No doubt in my mind this moose was the best meat I have ever eaten. This was one fun trip, but I don't need another one.

Moose and Dall sheep from Alaska. Elk from Montana.

In the 60s, Trinity Bible College was located in Jamestown. By this time we needed two full time employees on the farm plus extra summertime help. I never worried about workers. I said, "Lord, its yours, help me in ways to serve You and give to charities, church and missions," which has always been a big part of our giving. It so happened I've always had help on the farm.

Now Wesley Loven, who lived just two miles west and one/half south, our brother in law, had come on board for full-time employment. As I mentioned earlier, Gene and Shirley Wolff were living on the Everding farm and he was employed full time. For part-time help, we had students from Trinity, like Darryl Wileman, Bob Bachman and Allen Fercho who had farm backgrounds and could pitch right in. Darryl could see a problem and fix it. Bob was a good steady man, got a lot done, and Allen was OK too. Earl Fercho, Allens dad, came out a few days and adjusted our grain drill seeder.

One good man from Trinity Bible College was Mick Hessler. Mick did some scraper work for us with a six yard scraper and a 4020 John Deere tractor working in Jamestown and out on the farm. One day he got a little too aggressive and rolled over the scraper. No damage done, really, we set it back up and Mick kept on working.

We had one Trinity boy from New York City. He was a character. We brought him out from town Sunday night. When we got outside city limits he asked, "Where are the lights?" When he got out of bed Monday morning he asked, "Where are the houses?" He had never seen open range country. Then I told him to fill the grain seeder. He put fertilizer in the seed box and seed in the fertilizer box. To tell the truth, I don't think he knew what was seed and what was fertilizer. Then I put him on a tractor where he turned too short and bent the hitch. We took him back to town that night.

One day we had a bad windstorm. It blew the flax swaths and rolled them up into piles large enough to plug the feeder house on the combine. To harvest the flax, I went to Trinity, got four guys out and gave them each a pitchfork. I drove the combine from pile to pile and those guys forked in the flax. After two days of that they were glad we finished.

During the 60s was also the time David Sjostrom, our nephew, worked for us five summers while he was in high school and college.

It was always fun to have him around. It was the beginning of a life-long involvement. Years later I have heard him say he would call for money to keep going to study for the ministry. The joke is he didn't say how many times he called. Yes, it was all O.K. We were always glad we could help. After college we were invited to the wedding of David and Connie Nickell and we have been good friends ever since.

The year 1968, January 10th, our third child blessed us. Jeania was born in Jamestown hospital. What a perfect healthy little girl. It was kind of like starting over. It had been nine years after Jeffrey was born. My brothers teased me. They wondered at my age of 42 what I was thinking. They said I would never live long enough to see her graduate from high school. Well I sure fooled them. Not only did I see her graduate from high school, but from college too. I also walked her down the church aisle and saw her get married at age 35 in the year 2003. Yes, the Lord has blessed us with good health and long life.

MIRACLE 18 It was one of these earlier years, probably 1968-1970 the Lord awarded me a new Ford pickup. I say that because there were times when money was short, we were maintaining our pledges to the missionaries, and yet it just seemed to work out that we could buy new vehicles as we needed them. We felt everything we possessed was a hand down from God.

Driving out his new Ford I decided to go out in the country for a little drive. It was just before dark, got down the highway 15 miles and the new Ford stopped. It was 12 to 15 degrees below zero and I wasn't dressed heavy enough to start walking. If I sat there till morning I would have been a solid ice cube. Thank the Lord an Angel drove up in four door sedan, stopped and told me to get in. This Angel took me to my house, I got out, and It drove away never to see It again. Often we think Angels are only spiritual beings up in the clouds somewhere. We are made earthy and Gods hand can just as well be earthly too.

"Honor thy father and thy mother that thy
days may be long upon the land which
the Lord thy God giveth thee" (Exodus 20:12).

In May 1968, Bob and Sharon Unterseher graduated from Trinity. I had put a "help wanted" ad on the bulletin board of Trinity. Bob answered the ad, and right out of school we made a deal and he began a relationship that went far beyond that summer of work and is very current today.

Bob was the kind of guy that just grows on you. He did a good job. He was always interested in why we were doing a certain project. This particular summer we had other fellows on the farm too. One of them liked to talk a lot. Bob would often get frustrated and arguments would break out. I laughed more times listening to those two argue. One time it got really hot and I thought one might take the first swing. Bob finally walked away. One morning Bob came to work without the other guy. I asked, "Bob, how are you doing this morning?" He responded, "PEACE, PEACE, PEACE". Ironically that summer we had three Montana boys on the job. Each morning at 7:O'clock we would gather at the shop to get instructions for the day. These Montana guys would start right in with jokes about North Dakota. Finally, I asked one day, "If you Montana guys are so smart, why did you come to North Dakota to get your education?" That was the end of their jokes. Bob will surface in this book several times.

If some of my workers wanted to talk, they would shut down their tractors in the middle of the field and run across a quarter of a mile to someone else just to talk. Some ran high with legs forward.

We called them turkeys. The men would always tease someone. It was done in fun.

Now in farming there is a slack period between seed-time and harvest of about six weeks. This was the time of year I hooked up two 5020 John Deere tractors to dirt scrapers and helped build mobile home parks. As I mentioned, we started Capital Park in Bismarck in 1966. In 1968 I sent two men over to haul dirt and level the ground. One day it rained, the guys couldn't work. I had a call that day from the John Deere dealer in Bismarck. He said your men are in here wanting to trade off your equipment for newer and bigger things. The dealer asked me if they had authority to do this and if I would approve!!! That was one deal I shut down.

One day Fern drove to Bismarck to bring a man back for the weekend. As the man was driving and talking he struck a deer with the car. He was in the middle of a story and kept on driving and talking till he got done with the story and then decided to turn around, go back three miles, and see what happened to the deer. That was the style of that man. I soon made a change and put David Sjostrom and Wesley Loven on the job. We did this work building parks with the farm equipment for several summers.

Darryl Wileman, who worked for us on the farm two years, had a daughter Linda who was the same age as Jeania. They were together in Sunday school classes and played together a lot. As Linda grew up and went to college and then to China as a missionary, we were able to help support her. Later she married Steve Lilly and we are glad we can still help support them in China today.

Business was still growing and the Lord was blessing. In 1969 we were able to buy another 480 acres known as the Rasmussen

Picture of Mom and Dad shortly before Dad got sick with cancer.

farm. Mr. Rasmussen was not done working, maybe just wanted to pull out his equity. He was one of our good main employees for many years. Seemed like he was in love with the 875 Versatile tractor. He took good care of it and kept it clean.

The year of 1969 gave us a trip we will never forget. Pastor and Mrs. Miller, Ez and Marguerite, our mother Clara and Fern and I went to the Holy Land. We got to see the many places where Jesus walked. Traveled on the Red Sea, the Sea of Galilee and crossed the river Jordan. We also went through the eye of the needle. We attended a service at the wailing wall of Solomon's Temple. Accommodations were different, especially eating. Both Pastor Miller and Ezra contracted stomach flu from leafy salads that kept them in their room a couple days. Our mom at age 75 kept up with us all day long, walking and riding or whatever. It was great to tour the land where Jesus had lived and grown up from His childhood.

On Christ, the solid rock, I stand;
All other ground is sinking sand.

Edward Mote, 1863

No one can lay any foundation other than
the one already laid, which is Jesus Christ.

1 Corinthians 3:11

While over in Israel, we took a bus tour down into Egypt. We got to see the Great Pyramids and the Sphinx. Oh, what splendor! We rode over the Nile River and saw the farm production as they farm there. They mostly used hand and oxen labor, but great products. We rode camels in the hot scorching desert. We stood on the east banks of the Mediterranean Sea, and observed the Phoenician ruins area. On this same trip we toured Rome. We were at St. Peters Square. We saw where the Pope lives. We were in

St Paul's Cathedral. We saw the great Coliseum where Christians were persecuted. All of these areas are mentioned in the Bible.

During the period of Sherry and Jeff going to Montpelier School I was elected to the school board for two three-year terms, and was also PTA president for two years. I did a little political service, being precinct committeeman for several years. Sherry had a classmate, Susan Johnson. The Johnson farm was south of us. Through a long story, and Susan staying overnight with us, we were finally offered the privilege of picking up the Johnson children for Sunday school. Susan's sister Marilyn was older and Brian and Allen were younger. This was always fun to go the extra 10 miles and take them along to church. The two girls were real faithful in going and the boys went at least half the time. The girls' grandma lived in Jamestown and sometimes they went to her place after church and sometimes we kept them with us and we would buy them dinner or take them with us to Mom's house for Sunday dinner. Sometimes in winter when the roads were blocked with snow, we took a different route to pick up the Johnson kids, which was 12 miles extra one way. One person from the church asked why we would drive all those extra miles just to take kids to Sunday school. The children couldn't help that we had snowstorms, and being in a home where they didn't go to church they needed help. This is another beginning of a story that doesn't end here. Watch for Marilyn's name down the line. The Lord's blessings were great.

We would also like to think this was the beginning of a spiritual foundation for the late Major Allen Johnson. Allen moved out west to Yakima, Washington to be close to his sister Marilyn. While out there he married and had a family. He also joined the National Guard. Unfortunately Allen was chosen to serve in the war in Iraq.

He would have completed his term over there in March, 2007. He was killed the last part of January. We were able to attend the memorial service in Jamestown at the First Methodist Church February 9th, 2007. The testimonies of his spiritual witness where outstanding. One of his buddies in Iraq came back to bear witness of this fact as he spoke of Allen at the funeral. Allen was a spiritual witness to his comrades. His passing was a great lose to all of us.

"Jesus said, suffer the little children to
come unto me, and forbid them not for
of such is the kingdom of God" (Mark 10:14).

In 1970, a new idea came along. JES formed a partnership with Carl and Gertrude Mueller to build Kirkwood Apartments in Bismarck. Carl was to be the driving force. A total of 180 units were built on that property. Later on another piece of ground was converted to an additional 45 units.

By this time we were building Park Apartments in Jamestown, which ended up with 144 units. The Jamestown units were managed and operated by Wayne Monson.

Wayne and Carl were both very dedicated men. Carl was with us for 20 years, contracted cancer and passed away. Gertrude continued management several more years. Wayne has been with us 34 years and retired in 2006 at age 80.

A friend and business partner of later years made a speech I haven't forgotten. Lloyd Hansen, having residences in Florida and Norway, and we have the privilege of serving on the Amity board together, talked about how important connections are and that the Lord keeps leading us to the right people. We need to be attentive to opportunities, but the Lord will lead us. That has surely been the case with Fern and I and also JES. If you notice as this story goes on we have been blessed many times over, by meeting the right people at the right time. There are many good connections yet to come.

"For I know the plans I have for you,
declares the Lord, plans to prosper you
plans to give you hope and a future"
(Jeremiah 29: 11).

I must say my early right contacts were my brothers Ezra and Silas. As I stated before, Ezra helped me get started farming back in 48-49. This gave me a start so I could help Silas buy farmland. The greatest achievement was when we formed JES, which has lasted to this day. Ezra, because of his growing family, divided out some parts of the business, but has still been a partner in many apartments and in farming. Reuben, my brother and his wife Clarice have also joined us in apartment and farm real estate ventures.

Reuben and Clarice have been farming parts of our land for 40 years, starting with the Erickson farm. They have been very generous to work with. When we sold our farmstead at Montpelier, I began parking equipment at their farm headquarters and kept small tools and supplies in their shop. This has been a big blessing, saving me lots of miles and knowing our equipment had some protection. I want to give them special recognition at this place in this book. THANK YOU, THANK YOU!

Through the years, Silas and I worked together the most. Inside JES, Silas was a good connection for me. Although he is sharper and quicker than me, we were always able to work and play together. We did many things together including flying our twin-engine airplane. We airlifted men and supplies to our South Dakota farm operation for three years, landing that twin engine airplane at Pierre, South Dakota many times. Our 1000-acre farm

Main farm service truck, Arthur used for service in South Dakota.

was only 20 miles east of Pierre.

In 1971, JES was able to buy the Schultz farm which consisted of 320 acres.

This was an interesting approach. Mr. Schultz said he had tried to sell the farm through the FHA and Bank Finance systems and nothing came together. I told him we would pay cash. He said we had more power than either of the other systems. Really, I think the Lord was just saving it for us.

One more time I had to think of my walk
"out behind the barn."

In 1972 we rented the Walter Piehl farm. This was a good 800-acre piece of ground. Walter had signed a five-year contract at $12.00 per acre, which was okay for then. Soon after signing this contract, land rents began to go up. I know Walter felt badly. I paid him extra money each year in accordance with the times. We created a friendship that has never quit. We farmed his farm for 30 years and enjoyed it. I never felt right taking advantage of them just because we had a five year contract. I am sure we wouldn't have had the farm for 30 years if I hadn't paid more than our contract called for. Walter and Hattie were great people. Every year or two they joined us at a steak house for dinner. Four different times we met in Mesa, Arizona, in the wintertime. What great camaraderie! Walter always paid, unless somehow I could sneak the ticket away from him. We had the pleasure of having them in our home also.

We were still sending combines south for the harvest in Kansas. Some of the workers for a few years were Chris and Llewelyn Paulson. Cris was in his late 60s, but tough as nails. His son Llew was young and single, but got married and brought Betty along too. Then there was Lyle Vilhauer and Dan Rueb who both were good operators. The middle 70s is the time when Sherry and Jeff were the right age for harvest work. Jeffrey got an early start driving combine. At 12 years of age, I would let Jeff get into the cab of the combine. He knew how to start and stop the machine. If any little thing went wrong he was to toot the horn, never getting out to fix it. I was always near enough, it was a safe thing. Jeff's Mom didn't like the idea too well.

In Sherry and Jeffrey's Junior and Senior year, Fern and I loaded up the combines pulled by one truck each. Jeff and I each drove a truck pulling a combine on a trailer. Mom and the girls drove the new 4-door pickup with fuel tank and service supplies. Lyle Vilhauer was along as combine operator. Lyle and Jeff drove the combines, Sherry moved trucks in the field to keep up for filling with wheat, and I hauled the grain to town. Sherry seemed to catch on fast to truck driving. She wasn't afraid to push down the peddle and get things moving. It wasn't the best for Jeania, who was 8-10 years old. She broke out from wheat dust allergies. Mom was the morale builder with all the good sandwiches, snacks and pop.

The worst area for cutting wheat was around Kiowa, Kansas, where the soil below black topsoil was a yellow clay. It never failed that we would get a big cloudburst of rain. Trucks and combines both would sink in to the axles. When that clay dried it was on to stay. The farmer always kept a big farm tractor in the field to pull us out of the mud.

My memory fails me as to which two years we joined forces with Virgil Gerig to go combining. He had a semi-trailer that would haul two combines. He hauled one of our John Deere combines and I took the other with a single axle truck and trailer. Chris and Llew Paulson made both these trips along with Darwin Verke. These were pretty good years. Virgil had good large farm customers to cut for.

On one of these combine trips, pulling into Pratt, Nebraska, I stopped to go into a store to buy some socks. It was early in the morning, just as the stores were opening up for the day. I picked out the socks I wanted, paid the clerk, grabbed the package and went out to the field to combine. That evening we checked into our motel. My brother Paul, who was along on this trip, asked me what that bag of money was doing up on the back window of the car. I asked, "What bag?" Paul said, "There is a bag of money out there." Upon examining the bag, I found I had picked up the money bag the clerk had intended to put into the till. I went in the next morning and returned the money. As the merchant had no idea who I was or where I was working, he thought the money was gone. The merchant asked what he could do for me. I said, "Nothing, except maybe some popularity." Two days later this story came out over national news. My neighbor, George Herman

Jr. up in North Dakota verified this. He had heard it on national news.

Around 1972, JES started building a park in Devils Lake. Taking farm tractors to start excavation of soil, Henry Rassmusen and Marvin Lee drove the 5020 tractors up to the site. Wesley Loven drove up the pickup with fuel and supplies. They worked every day except Sunday to get done before freeze up. After cutting through a twelve foot hill and moving one-half of it we got done in good time. We built 120 spaces there.

In 1974, we had a chance to trade in a farm on the purchase of a mobile home. This was a 600-acre farm near Eureka, South Dakota. We rented out this farm to a local farmer. We later enrolled this farm into the government CRP program. JES also bought another 700 acres and rented 300 more at Blunt, South Dakota. We farmed there, moving equipment from our Montpelier farm. This was about the time that Jeff and Kenis Loven, Jeff's cousin, and Wesleys son, were old enough to drive tractors. They would start at 6 o'clock in the morning and before dark they would be down to Blunt, 250 miles from home. It sounds like a drag but listening to their stories, they killed gophers and birds and counted rabbits on the way.

This was about the time Arthur, Le Anne and Shannon Duncklee came to work on the farm. Shannon was three years old when he offered to bless our lunch. As he started praying Duke, the dog, barked and Shannon said "shut-up Duke" and then he finished his prayer.

It seemed as though Arthur was the right man for the job. He and Le Anne, our nephew and niece, moved into the second house on our farm. Now I thought I had a man for the next 20 years. As we had just purchased a farm in South Dakota, I decided to go to an auction sale. They had a service truck, complete with air compressor, two welding machines, rear end hoist, and power winch up front, which I knew would be ideal for traveling to our farm in South Dakota.

Just two winters later, while we were still in Florida, we received a call from Le Anne. "When are you coming home and can we take you out for dinner" she asked. Little did we know it was their way of informing us they planned to leave the farm. And I thought "why now" it's just time to start the spring seeding.

We farmed this South Dakota land during three dry years and lost faith in the project. I had a weak moment and we sold the farm. It was a mistake, as right after this time USDA started the CRP program. We should have enrolled the farm in that.

It was a jolt to receive the word at first, that Arthur and Le Anne were leaving, but soon the Lord provided two other men. Doug Ely and Terry Ost both stayed about 12 years until we had a sale and rented out the farm. Doug was a good man, sharp with weed chemicals and fertilizer. He could get a lot done in a short time if he put his mind to it. Terry was good with trucks, both driving and repairing. He could take out a truck engine, repair it, and install it back in again. He also made many trips to Fargo hauling sunflowers with a truck and two Farm Pup trailers, which we had built.

> The future doesn't belong to the fainthearted;
> it belongs to the brave.   Ronald Reagan

In the summer of 1974 we decided to take the family to Alaska in our 30-foot motor home. Now, as I said before, we always like to have others with us when we travel. We asked Amy Liechty, Bob and Sharon Unterseher and their two children to go along. That made 10 of us in an 8X30-foot motorhome. The ladies said

Farm Pup trailers designed by Jon.

that wasn't enough privacy and we decided to pull a little fold down Starcraft camper. We left Jamestown around 4:00 PM. And set up our first camp in Carrington. Bob and Sharon and there two children slept in the fold down camper. The wind blew hard during the night. It was cold. The furnace didn't work. That was the last night they slept in the trailer. All ten of us slept and traveled in the motor home from that day on. By the third day, we were on the muddy Alaskan Highway. Tires throwing mud all day knocked the wheel wells out of the little camper, and there was mud all over the inside. Bob and Sharons clothes were an awful sight. On dry days the wheels pumped dust inside. We still had to pull that camper the rest of the way up and back. One day a truck driver following us shouted on the CB radio, "Your trailer is on fire". Both wheel bearings went out and the camper was smoking. I had to hitch hike to the nearest town and buy new bearings. We finally made it to Skagway, where Gil and Mildred Meroney lived. It was a real treat to be with them and kind of regroup and clean up. Plus the Meroneys had ample supply of crab, fish and elk meat on hand. Man, was that food good! Gil was good at the outdoor grill and Mildred knew how to season food. We went looking at old gold mines and ice glaciers. Gil had a four-seat Cessna airplane. He took us up over the canyons and glaciers. Talk about a vast wilderness of ice and beauty, it was terrific. Gil also showed us how to set traps for crabs under water. We caught a large one that is somewhat like the one mounted in our office, plus we caught a few small ones too.

We got refreshed and made a loop up to Fairbanks and the city of North Pole. Our niece and nephew, LeAnne and Arthur Duncklee, now in the air force, lived there. It was fun to see this place with nature at its fullest. We saw moose, bear, deer, elk and a great variety of birds at close range in this area. Then we came back to Haines City where we drove our motor home and camper onto a huge ferry that took us back to Vancouver, BC. Scenery on the ferry coming back was beautiful. To see the bald eagles soar high above the waters and watch the wild animals run were very interesting. After getting back on land in Canada, we drove through rich fruit and farm country in Alberta. Driving home

Trip to Alaska with Bob Untersehers taken at North Pole, Alaska

through Montana we stopped for gas and groceries. Leaving town, about 4 miles out we found Jeania was missing. Talk about horror and hollering at that point. All I heard was, "Jon, turn this motor home around!" Of course I knew I wanted to, but couldn't turn till we got to the next exit. We drove back to that gas station and found Jeania safe. A clerk at the store had assured her we would be back. Actually, Jeania was only looking at all the kinds of candy in the store, when we drove off. Each one of us felt guilty that she was left. We did all come home as friends and really enjoyed the whole trip. Bob and Sharon were fun to travel with. If you keep reading you'll find this wasn't our last trip with them.

One more big event took place in 1973. That Sunday school girl, Marilyn Johnson, whom we helped through Trinity Bible College, was ready to get married. While at college she met this Yakima Valley cowboy, Tim Waddington. We had heard about this after school started in August and on November 30th they were married. The wedding was nice. They were a good match for each other.

The Waddingtons were a musical family. Tim would take his guitar, play and sing, and always draw a crowd. After marriage, Tim felt a call of the Lord to get into some type of ministry. Coming from a family of 19 children, Tim always had brothers and sisters who would make up a musical team and travel through towns and churches, holding concerts and speaking. They did this for several years and then the children started coming. It was always a joy to have them pull into our yard and spend a day or two. One day Tim and Marilyn drove in with two of his sisters, Miriam and Carolina. The two girls went into our downstairs bedroom and slept all night and with no windows in the room they didn't realize time was going on. They missed breakfast and lunch, coming out of their room at four o'clock the next afternoon. It seemed funny at the time. We usually tried to feed them and fill their big bus gas tank before they left.

Finally the family got bigger, to a point, where they needed more room. Tim was able to buy a big diesel bus. It was interesting to fill that machine, 150 or more gallons at a time. He formed a board of directors and put me into one position on the board. Conrad Twedt also was on the board. We would meet at various places where Tim would minister and try to help. Tim and Marilyn believed that,

"God so loved the world that He gave His only
begotten Son that whosoever believed on Him
should not perish but have everlasting life" (John 3:16).

Taking used school buses and making them into Sunday school buses was all the rage in the 1970s. We had become friends with a school bus dealer in Fargo. He would sell us his used buses at reasonable prices. Now remember, we had our nephew, David Sjostrom, work for us summers while in college and now he was a pastor in the state of Washington.

David knew who needed buses. I would buy them in Fargo and find drivers to take them west and David would sell them out there. We never made much money but had reasons to drive out west to visit and help some churches. Bob Unterseher drove sometimes. One time we took three buses as far as a men's retreat in western Montana. Three men came from Washington and drove them the rest of the way. We always worked some fun around each trip. At this Montana retreat, there were hot springs of water so we would bathe in the pools and then take a roll out in the snow. Talk about anything crazy, we did it. We even sewed Bob's pajamas shut one time, among other crazy things.

One of four pink snoopy buses running for Sunday school while David and Connie were youth pastors in Jamestown.

Family pictures in early 70s.

Nine
BUSINESS AND TRAVEL

Farm Pup trailer built to add payload behind a bobtail truck.

Another project of the middle 70s was building the Farm Pup Trailers. Back in those years most farm trucks were single axle trucks, which only allowed them to haul three to four hundred bushels of grain. I devised a hopper bottom trailer that hauled another 300 and 400 bushels along with the truck. It was like hauling two loads to the elevator in one trip.

The Farm Pup trailer seemed to catch on well and sales were increasing. We were building them in our farm shop. It was taking more shop room. We had hired two men as part-time welders. We asked ourselves, "Should we build another shop, and if so, on the farm or in town?" We had put out around 50 trailers and had a chance to sell our idea, our jigs, and drawings to a machine manufacturer in Fargo. We were to get royalties on each trailer they built. The new company was beginning to grow when President Nixon put on an embargo on sales to Russia. This brought wheat prices from $5.00 per bushel down to $3.00, causing sales of the trailer and other products the new company was building, to nothing. The company filed bankruptcy. That was the end of the Farm Pup Trailer. As time passed, farms got larger and semi-tractor trailers replaced smaller trucks.

Somewhere in the mid 70s our family and some of Leo and Dorothy Miller's family, our super pastors of 20 years, got together and took a MAPS trip to Brussels, Belgium. Melvin and Eleanor Jorgenson were the missionaries in charge at that time. Our duties were to work on a French Chateau, which had been purchased by the Assemblies of God. We did cement work, sheet rocking, painting and some woodwork. It was my chance to learn a new skill, sheet rocking. It was very interesting and it gave me confidence to do my own house. Food was basically good and with plenty of it. Their milk was kept on the shelf, not in the refrigerator and the taste was really different. After our two weeks work there, we rented a large nine-passenger van and started driving north. We entered Germany. Leo did real well with the German language and I could speak a little. We stayed at bed and breakfast deals as much as possible.

Traveling north we drove through Denmark and into Sweden, the ancestry of both Fern and Dorothy. Now it was their turn to guide us, as they both spoke Swedish. First thing the girls did was kiss the ground of Sweden. As far as speaking the language, the dialects were so different, they couldn't understand one another. It was disappointing because Fern had distant relatives there but was unable to communicate or locate them. Fern even had a phone number to call, but couldn't communicate enough to be able to locate them. We enjoyed good Swedish coffee and food just the same. The style of dress wearing knee length skirts and knee high stockings were very unique, something like a Bavarian style of dress.

From Sweden we drove into Norway. We spent a day in the beautiful fjords, traveling up and down the shores and visiting sights and small shops. I purchased a Norwegian sweater. We turned in our van at this point and flew out of Norway back to the United States.

Sherry graduated from high school in 1976. Sherry was a good singer and staged a couple of concerts that summer. She had musical background with her cousins, Amy Liechty, at the piano, her brother Steve played the drums, and Jeff on the bass guitar. Amy also played saxophone. Four kids from our church, Amy Liechty, Andrea Miller, Kenis Loven (another cousin) and Jeffrey Liechty all played saxophone. Jeff played a big Bass Berry Sax. The four of them entered competition, won state and went on to nationals in Oklahoma City. OK. It was great for them.

I was Sunday school superintendent at First Assembly of God Church in Jamestown. Having held that position for several years, we invited the Sunday school staff out to our farmhouse for a picnic and monthly meeting. As people drove out they commented how nice the fields of waving grain looked. There was a nice crop coming. We had a good meal and the staff left our house at 11:00 p.m. At 12:00 o'clock it started raining and hailing. The hailstorm of 1976 was one of the worst on record. It pounded holes through our garage roof and destroyed one of our three old barns. There were no leaves left on the trees. They were stripped clean with only stub branches left. Later our friends from Nebraska, the George Studlers, our combine customers, remarked about what funny looking trees we grew. Crops were totally gone. Out of 3,000 acres of wheat there were 80 acres worth trying to harvest. Whoa! No harvest meant no crop and no paycheck for one whole year. "Lord," we prayed, "how can we keep up our support to the 15 missionaries we wrote checks to each month and the church and Sunday school support?" Was this Job's test for us? While we had this JES partnership going we tried to keep each enterprise separate to make its own way. Now I was manager of the agriculture department which meant I needed to go look for my own money and survival. Fern and I stood on the Scripture that says,

"And be content with such things as you have;
for he hath said, I will never leave thee, nor
forsake thee" (Hebrews 13:5).

I also knew my walk "out behind the barn" would not fail. This test was maybe good for Fern and I and the family, but it was tough. During this time we bought old cars. We had to stay home more, budget our eating and special events. We didn't want to fail the people we were supporting.

We had good favor with our banker, Mr. Buegel. We were able to get money enough to keep up with all our missionary pledges and support to the church. We tried to keep a positive attitude and that kept us going. Through all this, God was faithful and we knew:

"All things work together for good, (food,)
to those that love God" (Romans 8:28).

Life wasn't all bad. In 1976 I celebrated my 50th birthday. That year my birthday, July 18th, fell on a Sunday. I took my first real motorcycle ride to church on my birthday. On my way to church I passed Lyle Sjostroms farm. Lyle was mowing grass along the road, so I stopped and had a chat with him. We still talk about my first ride on the cycle. To celebrate, I tried golfing for my first time. Jeff had been learning to fly airplanes the past two years and I began trying a little flying after I was 50. I got my private pilot license in 1978. After Jeff and I got our license, we bought our own Cessna 172, a black and white Sky Hawk. This was a very forgiving airplane. I could fly over farm fields, land on roads, check crops and get back home in a hurry. I remember while farming in South Dakota, 250 miles away, we ran out of sunflower seed while seeding. We threw a few bags of seed into the Sky Hawk and airlifted seed to South Dakota.

Our Cessna 172 airplane

With the assistance of Lyle Sjostrom and his expertise we put lights on a runway at the farm with the on/off switch in the house. If I left and didn't get back before dark I could call home and tell them to turn on the runway lights. One time Fern, Jeania and I took the laundry to town after dark in the plane.

The year we farmed Tom and Jeannette Waldie's farm, twenty miles away, the plane was real handy. The Waldies had a good grass runway on their farm, which made it handy to check on operations there. One day I flew down to Waldies to check on the combines and tried to land on a gravel road in a strong wind. The air was real squirrelly. I landed on the road and just as I hit ground the plane turned onto an approach and stopped 20 feet from the combine. I am sure I had help from above that time.

The plane was also handy to carry my golf bag. I would land at Waldies' farm and Larry Johnson would pick me up and we would golf at Grand Rapids, N.D. I would fly to Kulm and Lonnie Titus and I would golf nine holes and have lunch, other times we flew to Oakes and golfed with Harvey Wolff.

One day Jon Nitschke called. He couldn't find some cattle. We went up in the plane and spotted them. It was a real windy day with 40 MPH winds when we came back into Jamestown. I asked Jon if he thought we could land in the wind. He wasn't used to flying, he turned white as a sheet.

Two different occasions, in the 172 Cessna, Darryl Justesen accompanied me to different areas of North Dakota to contact farmers about buying some of Concords new equipment.

Another time, with our 172 Cessna, I went to sell some equipment to a farmer 100 miles away. I called Mr. Johnson about a place to land, he responded, right in front of the house, spray planes land here all the time. He didn't tell me he had a mail box along the driveway. I landed and saw the mail box coming at me, I pulled back on the wheel, gave it full throttle and cleared the mail box. By this time there were trees in front of me. I made it over the trees at a steep angle and then the plane stalled out on me. I landed in a corn field with some prop damage but I didn't get a scratch or a bruise. They say any landing you walk away from is a good landing. I am not so sure!

I must tell you about our Canadian fishing trips. During the late 70s I would take Jeffrey, Silas took his son, Curtis, Ezra took his son, Wayne, and Reuben took his son, Richard. We would fill our three airplanes and head for Canada. Reuben had a four-place Cessna 182RG which hauls four, our Sky Hawk held four and the twin engine Barren belonging to Liechty Homes, which Si flew, was a six passenger, totaling 14 seats to fill. There were eight of us. The other seats would go to Lyle Sjostrom and his son, Todd, Larry Johnson, Pastor Leo Miller, Kenny Wurgler and one of his sons, or Milton Rolle and his son, Darrin. Milton would bring along the breakfast, in a skillet, stirred up with eggs over potatoes, sausage and onions, MAN, a meal fit for a king! You couldn't buy a breakfast that good any where. The loads weren't always the same. We would mix-match passengers always having full loads. We would fly up early morning, catch and eat all the fish we could, returning with our limits at the end of the third day. This was done every year for five or six years. Viewing the many miles, in all directions, over many countries, you are reassured:
"The earth is the Lord's and the fullness thereof"(Psalm 24:1).

We got to know our friends, Larry and Jeanette Johnson, while farming at Montpelier. Larry was the manager of the Marion Equity Elevator. I began hauling grain there in the 60s. Larry was always ready for a cup of coffee. Very seldom did I ever go there and not visit the café for coffee. Our friendship grew as time went on. When selling grains to the elevator, I would tell Larry he was paying too much. He'd say, "It's not enough." Larry was a man who cared for his customers. As mentioned before, I believe he went on every fishing trip to Canada. We hunted pheasants together for many years, including one trip to the Schauer Brothers farm at Mott, N.D. Steve Dale was along on this trip too.

I couldn't tell you how many times Larry and I played golf together. We went to places like Grand Rapids, Enderlin and LaMoure, North Dakota. We also golfed at Wyndmere, North Dakota after they moved there.

One time Larry and Jeanette, Si and Martha, and Fern and I flew our Beechcraft Baron to the Winnebago factory and drove two new motor homes back to Jamestown. On another trip we met Larry and Jeanette at Green Bay, Wisconsin and attended a Packers game.

The Johnsons came to Florida to visit us and we went to Texas and stayed with them in their home. They were great entertainers.

Larry retired from Marion Equity Elevator. He began showing signs of Parkinson's disease. We kept in touch right up to the end of his life. We were in Florida and got back in time to see and pray with him just two days before he died. I asked him if he was going to see Jesus, and he brightened up and responded in a positive way the best he could in his frail condition. He was truly a friend.

One more flight I must tell you about. When President Reagen came to Grand Forks, North Dakota to help Mark Andrews campaign for US Senate I was interested in going. Our pastor, Darrell Losing, is interested in politics, so he and I decided to fly up and take in the rally. I was talking to the tower on a hazy morning as we approached Grand Forks, and they were guiding us in and had me on their radar, they said. I told them I had the runway in sight and they cleared me to land. Evidently they weren't watching closely enough and I landed at the United States

Air Force Base with Air Force One sitting on the tarmac. That set off a lot of commotion. They told me to stop at once. They came out with armored vehicles and led us into headquarters. They had us get out of our plane into their vehicle and hauled us in. We were questioned for about 20 minutes and then they let us fly out again. I think they were having fun. We were not. We did get in on part of the rally for Mark Andrews and heard part of Reagans speech. Also that day we met Pastor Paul Kyle of the Grand Forks Assembly of God Church. He drove us around town.

Some years later another interesting political event took place when George W. Bush came to Jamestown, ND. Pastor Losing, Silas and I had the pleasure of meeting him and shaking his hand. This was before he became governor of Texas, and of course now he is our President.

I guess Jeff can be thanked for getting me interested in flying. He got his private flying license in 1976. That was great for Jeff. And then he encouraged me and said, "Dad, I know you can do it also".

Nineteen seventy-six was also the year Sherry graduated from Montpelier High School. That fall she enrolled in North Central Bible College. Taking Sherry and all her belongings in our four-door Chevy pick-up, Mom and I left our poor little girl off in a big, big city. Although she did fine in her classes, we never knew until years later how homesick she was. Had we known we would have done more to help our young daughter, Sherry.

The following year, 1977, Jeff graduated from Montpelier High School. He also enrolled at North Central Bible College that same fall, and that made it much easier for both of them.

The two of them were both in a musical group called "First Love", and they traveled with the group so we got to see them more often.

We need to give lots of credit for the children's development of musical abilities to Harvey Wolff. Harvey was the music teacher at Montpelier High School. He had our kids playing in band and singing in chorus. He had Jeff playing the big bass viol and Sherry singing solos, and in duets and trios. Hauling that big bass viol was a job. At first we laid it across the seats of our Ford car. One day we found and bought a New Yorker Chrysler. The big bass viol fit neatly in the big trunk. This New Yorker worked well as a family car for three years, then a disaster. I went to a church board meeting. About midnight, two miles from home the New Yorker caught fire. I walked home and called the Marion fire department. They brought out water hoses, started the gas motors, ready to put out the fire. Guess what, no water on the fire truck! People asked if we had a hot board meeting that started the fire.

During these years we got to know Harvey and his wife Carole better. Having been a farm boy, Harvey would come out and help at our farm when time permitted. As we got better acquainted, Harvey and I started golfing together. Later they moved to Oakes. This was a one hour and a half drive from our farm or 20 minutes by plane. I would fly down with the golf clubs, play a round, eat a good meal and fly home. We have kept in touch with the Wolffs ever since the 70s. We always meet for dinner and exchange Christmas gifts each year. We have many late night telephone visits. Fern says we don't say anything worthwhile and she can't go to sleep. As late as last year Harvey would drive up from Oakes to help me on the Piehl Farm. He was an easy keeper with his bag of carrots at his side for snacks. Harvey was one who took interest in soil types and tried to improve methods, reminding me of:

"Sow for yourselves righteousness

reap in mercy, break up your fallow ground for it is time to see the Lord till He comes and rains righteousness on you" (Hosea 10:12).

The year 1977 offered another challenge. Our church sent a group of men to Guatemala to help build a mission church. This was a fun group of people. The group included our leader, Bob Unterseher, Pastor Miller, Jack Wilkenson, Darrel Anderson, Doug Anderson, Reuben, Silas and me, along with men from other churches in N.D. We started by pouring a footing and then laying up cement blocks for walls. Twice a day we would go to what we called the PX, an army term for all kinds of foods and notions. Really it was just a " hole in the wall" store where we could get sodas, ice cream and candy. At least it was a break away from those heavy cement blocks. In two weeks we had the entire roof on, over those blocks of cement. The night before we left, the nationals had their first church service in the building. I had been bitten by some kind of bug, and my hands swelled up like a balloon. The guys said I spent a few delirious nights. I remember the ladies out back making tortillas, standing out under a tree among flies and bugs. That was something else, kind of dried up your appetite.

The reason I mentioned Jack Wilkenson is because we have become friends also. We have visited their home in Arizona and have been over to their farm for dinners and coffee. For our 50th wedding anniversary they had us over for dinner. Millie fixed a good fried chicken dinner with all the fixin's. When the chicken came around she saw me looking for a special piece. Millie asked, "What are you looking for, Jon?" I said, "A wing." She said, "Oh, I didn't fix the wings." Then with a little small talk about it,

Jack Wilkenson and I laying blocks for a church in Guatemala.

we went on with dinner. When we were leaving their house she handed me a paper bag. It had all the wings in it.

I heard Jack tell someone later in years how I had bought some of their farm and he said, "We're still friends." Jack and Millie have since moved off the farm, retiring in one of our rental properties.

Jack and Millie had lost their son, Jim, in a tractor farm accident. Jim and Kathy and Jeff and Sherry were all schoolmates at Montpelier High School. Kathy would come and stay over night with Sherry, she was always fun to have around. Jack and Millie decided to sell off a part of the farm and we were the first one contacted. We bought 320 acres.

One day a Kansas farmer and harvester, Adam Nusz, looking for work stopped to see us. We put him to work on our wheat fields. He needed a truck driver. We got our neighbor girl, Arlene Smith, to drive truck for him. It seemed to be going well. One day it began to rain and I thought I had better drive out to the field and see if they were still combining wheat. I found them both in the same truck cab. Neither of them were married. That was a successful ride. The next year they came back for harvest, married. After this, Adam changed their route and began going to California to harvest.

We more or less lost track of them, but seems once I hook up with someone good they always come back.

It was in the late 70s when Adam was having problems meeting combine payments. He approached us to buy out the remaining contract and then he would pay us. We put the combines on a new 5-year pay off for Adam by securing the note for him, thus making a lower annual payment that he could handle. It worked out well. Adam and Arlene will be back again.

"He that knoweth to do good
and doeth it not to him it is sin" (James 4:17).

In 1979 a new opportunity came by. We were offered and bought 1980 acres of the Virgil Rott farm. Why more local farmers did not buy this has always puzzled me, except for the fact that my early army experience (out in the Atlantic) with Jesus, and my walk "out behind the barn" were working. We had set a goal of giving 30% of our profits to charities by this time.

The summer of 1979 had everyone guessing. What do the kids have in mind now? One night in June, twelve midnight, Bill calls just to talk. I thought that sure is funny, wake me up from sleep and not say anything. He talked a while and then hung up. Two hours later, two O'Clock AM Bill calls again, can I marry your daughter Sherry, he finally got up courage enough to ask.

1979 was a year of notable memories. In June, Sherry was married to William Owen. What a beautiful wedding and what a beautiful bride. I don't know why, nothing against Bill, I just thought nobody was good enough for my daughter. I needed to apologize for some of my thoughts and statements. Bill has been a wonderful son-in-law. More than that, I appreciate how patient and kind he is with Sherry. He gives her the best.

In October we found ourselves flying to Lincoln, Nebraska, to meet the parents of Crystal Glass, Jeffrey's bride-to-be. Mom, Jeania and I boarded Reuben's 182 RG, as he flew us off to Lincoln. Jeffrey and Crystal were married December 15, 1979. I didn't have as hard a time with this knowing that Jeff could take care of things. Although the day he packed up his belongings from home to move away was a tearjerker.

Crystal is a good mate for Jeff and has been a great daughter-in-law. We love our kids' companions very much. Jeff and Crystal have given us two lovely grandchildren.

After the December wedding, Jeff and Crystal went back to Minneapolis to work. I had no idea that he would ever come back to the farm. All I could do was hope. We went through the winter, drove through Minneapolis going to and coming from Florida. There were no indications of Jeff wanting to farm.

One day in March I got a call. Jeff asked if I had a place for him on the farm. I was so overwhelmed, I could hardly believe it.

In April 1980, Jeff started his farming career. We put in the crop in April and May and by June, Jeff and Crystal thought they would like to take the combines south for harvest. They needed additional help, so they got Crystal's brother, J.L. Glass and his wife Cheryl, and Curtis Liechty to go. This was the crew.

They did a good job and the farming year was very successful. With Jeff living in Jamestown, he was able to bring extra help to the farm like Jeff Glass and Lyle Vilhauer. Here is Lyle again. He had been harvesting with Fern and me a few years earlier.

MIRACLE 19 I'm not sure which of these years it was, when Jeff was bringing in a load of wheat from the Piehl farm, a grasshopper in the cab got too much of his attention and the truck rolled over spilling a full load of wheat into the ditch. He wasn't going fast, luckily he didn't get hurt, there was not much damage on the truck and we got most of the wheat picked up.

Bill and Sherry had been working for Bill's brothers in Minneapolis after they were married. This brings up an interesting story. Bill's brothers had started a tool and die business in the basement of their house. They wanted to upgrade their equipment. Really, they needed a new $5,000 machine to be successful on a bid job. Fern and I loaned them the $5,000 and helped start a business that runs in the millions today. It was encouraging to see them prosper.

In 1981 Bill and Sherry moved back to the farm. Bill wanted to learn farming. This first year, he and Sherry decided to go combining. By this time we had hired Doug and Cindy Meyers at the farm, and they were living in a mobile home at the farm. Bill, Sherry, Doug, Cindy and here came Lyle Vilhauer again, making up the harvest crew. Bill and Sherry seemed to catch on to the swing of harvest and they did a good job. Bill still wonders why I ever turned him loose with half a million dollars worth of equipment and an open checkbook. He handled it well. Bill also took an interest in our fertilizer and chemical business. He had studied and passed the USDA chemical dealers test. This is a very difficult test.

You can see what a variety of people I had on the farm crew, and others I could mention, like Dan Rueb, Harvey Loven, Wayne Rolle, Darwin Verke and others. I must say the Lord always provided help for the farm. Sometimes I wondered who was coming next.

When I first started farming, and my walk "out behind the barn," I had tried to concentrate on how much I could put into charities and give away and help others. With this I let the Lord provide help on the farm and plug holes of disaster that could arise.

I would like to mention that this time period was the high light of my years of ministry as Sunday School Superintendent. I began in that office in 1965. My first years were under the leadership of our good Pastor Miller. In 1981 the church elected Rev. Jack Glass to be the new pastor. Pastor Glass was an energetic man with lots of ideas, he and myself sitting at Perkins, over a cup of coffee, came up with lots of new plans. It was during his tenure we took the Church and Sunday School Christmas celebration down to the Jamestown Civic Center for the next three years of event there. This was a thrilling accomplishment in my term of office.

"Whoever works his land will have plenty to eat, but the one who chases unrealistic dreams has no sense". (Proverbs 12:11).

⇒⇒ *Ten* ⇐⇐
A NEW PARADIGM OF BUSINESS

Nineteen eighty-two was the beginning of a new era in our harvest combine operations. I feel the Lord saw we were busy enough on the local level and He provided Christian help from here on out. Harvest costs are always a big part of the costs of farming. There is profit in custom harvesting, especially if you can work it around your own crops.

This picture represents 50 years of combining.

With Jeff being home to help, we had rented additional land to where we were farming twice as many acres. Amos Stoltsfus was another one of these guys that once acquainted with us, you never know when they might come back. We met Amos and his wife, Joy, when they were song leaders at a Gerald Derstine Revival in Leeds, North Dakota. Our Dad had met Derstine in Florida under his tent and convinced him to hold meetings in Leeds. That was back in the early 60s. We had become good friends. Here 20 years later Amos called and asked if he could take our combines harvesting to Kansas. Talk about a godsend, Fern and I were tired of the responsibility. Amos and his family operated the harvest for the next five years. Amos was a hustler and really kept things moving. Doors didn't always close on time but he got them closed the next time through.

There are always memories. While working on our crops, we had a two-week rainy spell. About three o'clock one Wednesday afternoon it got dry enough to combine. Wednesday night, being church night, we loaded up for church. I told Amos they could quit and come to church also. He spoke of that event many times and thought it great to be able to quit, after a two-week shut down for rain, and go to church and of course, we have never harvested on Sunday.

"Six days you shall labor and do all
your work, but the seventh day is
the Sabbath to the Lord your God.
On it you shall not do any work" (Exodus 20: 9-10).

During this era we had become especially close to Lonnie and Bonnie Titus. The Titus's pastored the Assembly of God Church at Kulm. If you remember, that was Fern's home church where we were married. It was just the right place to take a few hours off the farm and relax.

Having the Cessna 172 made it "double" fun. I'd load up my golf clubs, and of course Fern had her sisters and brothers there too. Although she never liked flying in small planes, she was always ready to fly to Kulm.

Lonnie would meet us at the airport and take me to the golf course, out to the sand greens. Sand greens are really different to putt on. That's where he would beat me. But he usually had a coffee jug and cookies along so I forgave him on the golfing. We would hook up with Roy Olson or some other banker or business friend of Lonnie's. Then there were plane rides they wanted, too. A few times Loren or Steven, my nephews, flew along to Kulm.

Lonnie did have some other goals in mind. He seemed to have a nitch to work and assist political figures in times of distress. I tried to assist his efforts and was able to introduce him to the governor of North Dakota, Allen Olson, and other figures around the capital I knew. Later after they moved to Minneapolis, we kept in touch. One winter they came to our home in Florida, where we helped them buy a car. Another time they bought a Dodge van from us. We always thought our money was wisely spent contributing to Lonnie and Bonnie. Another time we gave a Dodge mini van to the Lowell Lundstrom Ministries.

MIRACLE 20 Due to the fact that Sherry and Jeffrey had both attended North Central Bible College in Minneapolis, the college people knew where we lived. Their PR man and fundraiser Jack Strom called in 1982. He said apartment units adjacent to the college had come up for sale. They were the Orfield properties, consisting of five buildings, a total of 125 apartments. The Orfields wanted $250,000 down. Colleges don't have a lot of extra money, and being investors we don't keep that kind of money lying around either. We told Jack Strom we thought we could get the money.

It just so happened by this time JES had enough farmland paid off with clear title. We were able to secure money and make the loan to North Central Bible College. Don Argue, president at the time, was very appreciative. President Argue, with his integrity, had us all paid back in five years. About one year after the loan was made, I was asked to serve on the Board of Regents for the college. It has been a good education and fun assignment.

"Doing what is right and fair is more
acceptable to the Lord than offerings of sacrifice"
(Proverbs 21:3).

Fern's niece, Le Anne, and her husband, Arthur Duncklee, who had worked for us at the farm three years and now was in the military, were stationed in Scotland with the U.S. Air Force. It gave us a chance to go and spend a few days with them. They drove us to London and toured with us through the city and down under in the subway streets. We got to see the Queen's Palace, heard the clock on the Big Ben Towers strike, and of course all the pigeons were bombing the streets.

An opportunity for more farm real estate came in 1983. This land adjoined the Brown farm and was also part of the old Chicago Ranch, known as the Lee farm. Mr. Lee had 470 acres at this location that we wanted and he also had 320 acres that my friend Lyle, wanted. Needless to say, my friend and JES together made an offer and bought it all. Our part was 470 acres.

These friends, Lyle and Evelyn Sjostrom, had become acquainted with us back in the late 60s. Lyle was an employee of Otter Tail Power Co. and when we first met he was living in Holiday Park Village. Lyle bought a farm south of town and started more with cattle. I remember him asking to rent pasture ground. Later he rented some farm ground and we got more involved, then he started buying land. In the mix of all this we were using each other's machinery. Maybe he used more of mine. This is another case where our friendship never ends. In the early years I would do his combining. Lyle would come out after work at Otter Tail, ride with me and drink coffee. He also drove combine and truck for me on kind of a trade-off basis. Sometimes I charged him for work, but we always had fun working together.

One time Lyle and I were harvesting his flax. The flax was bunchy and would plug the combine. Flax is the worst straw to try to pull out of a plugged combine. We tore our nails and laughed and kept going.

One day I was helping Lyle in his yard. The chickens had spread manure on the machine we were working on. Lyle remarked that chickens were more of a nuisance than they were worth. In fun I said, "I wish I could afford some chickens." Later that year we went to Minneapolis, coming home the second day, arriving home after dark. The next morning about daylight, we heard roosters start crowing. They were noisy things. I commented to Fern, "I think, our neighbors, Art Mayers, (less than one half mile up the road), must have bought some roosters". Not so, Lyle had brought down 20 chickens and roosters. They were wild, they flew and roosted in the trees. Later in the fall we wanted to butcher them, but we couldn't catch them. Jeff and I each took rifles and tried shooting them. The target was pretty small for deer rifles. We managed to get five of them. We put four in the freezer and Mom tried cooking one. She cooked it about three hours and we still couldn't chew the bird. We kept them in the freezer till Christmas, wrapped them up in Holiday paper and gave them back to Lyle.

Another time, Evelyn commented that Lyle didn't wear pajamas. I bought him a good pair at Straus and gave them to him for Christmas. The next Christmas I got them back. I gave them to him the third year and they came back to me in year four.

Lyle wanted to use my new versatile tractor and 40-foot John Deere digger. Well, really I offered it to him. He didn't get far. Feeling badly he came back. The brand new tractor broke an axle before he got started in the field. He took me out late at night to show what had happened. He really hated to tell me. Luckily the tractor was still under warranty. It didn't cost either of us any money to fix it up. We owned a few pieces of equipment together and got along good. We also did a cattle-feeding venture together.

Lyle was a good electrician. We were continually putting up buildings for shops and grain-drying equipment. Lyle was always ready to do this work for me. He never once charged for his services.

The offset for us came when he rewired our whole farm base. We had wires hanging from pole to pole, some in bad shape and some broken. Lyle put all our wiring with new wires underground. It included the house, the well, the old shop and the new shop and the grain elevator and drying system. I mean it was first class.

⇒ *Eleven* ⇐
FRIENDSHIPS

One of the better parts of our friendship was the coffee times we had at Lyle and Evelyn's. It didn't matter what time of day it was, Evelyn never got shook up if we came in for coffee. In a few minutes the coffee was ready with something good to go with it. If she was busy, she just kept on working, otherwise she often had a cup too. She made me feel at home. On my way to town from the Montpelier farm it was so easy to swing into their farm. We would talk a few minutes and Lyle would say, "Let's go in for coffee." We always had some farm issue to talk about. One year we owned cattle together. Some years Lyle would fatten a steer calf, have it butchered and sell us some of that good meat. That was back in my selling days. I sold Lyle corn and sunflower seed. I also sold him his first Concord Air Seeder.

Whenever yard lights went out or we needed to go up high, he had the equipment to do it. I had bought five hopper bottom tanks from an elevator company. Lyle knew how to take them down and how to put them back up.

Like I mentioned before, Lyle always went fishing with us in Canada. One year, soon after we bought the park in Florida, they brought their three children to visit us in Florida. We traveled in a motor home to the beach and several of the attractions, including Bush Gardens. Fern took a ride on one of those deals where you hang up-side down and twirl around until you are so dizzy you can't stand up. In all of this ride, Fern lost her sense of smell. Too bad, she has not smelled a nice flower since. We do make the best of it by saying this may have saved our marriage. Fern can't smell anything and I can't hear anything.

As recent as 2003, Lyle and Evelyn came to Florida to stay with us. In turn we visited them in Arizona. They gave us a tour of their beautiful new home and we were served a big salad, potato, and steak dinner.

We were almost like brothers. He almost loved me as much as he loved himself.

Leviticus 19:18 says, "Love your neighbor as yourself." This was Lyle.

A new part of our business was formed in 1983. Concord Air Seeders was a new concept of farming. The part that makes it air seeding is the fact that behind the seeding tool is a large trailer tank which holds the grain seed and fertilizer. This product is moved from tank to seeder by high volumes of air flowing through tubes taking the metered amount of product with it. The seeder itself could be either a disc drill or shovel-type cultivator. Being new to the industry, there was lots of interest.

Jeff was helping at the farm at the time and helped us remodel our machine storage building into a big heated shop. It was a nice place to assemble equipment. With extra help we were able to set up enough machines to where we were one of the top dealers.

MIRACLE 21 Howard Dahl, president of Concord, made a trip to Florida to see Silas and me for assistance. The plan looked good, we discussed the venture and both decided to go for it. The Concord Company was growing so fast, they were looking for investors. They were looking for high volume help.

Being investors in farms and mobile home parks and now giving 40% of our profits to church and charities, we didn't have piles of money lying around.

I really believe the Lord saw this ahead of time. He had positioned a man in a large Fargo bank who had been a banker in our city, Jamestown, and he knew our character. (One more good connection). We were able to secure the entire funds with just our signature, no collateral.

I believe my Atlantic Ocean experience and my walk "out behind the barn" was a big influence for this deal, the best is yet to come.

"And my God will meet all
your needs according to his
glorious riches in Christ Jesus" (Philippians 4:19).

One more fun thing in 1984 was the trip to Portugal when we took our entire family on a MAPS program. We helped on construction of a Bible college complex. Working with cement blocks and cement mud buckets on the second floor was a man-sized job. The cement was pulled up in buckets by rope and pulley. The Duane Henders and the Sam Johnsons were our hosts. Soup and chow furnished by the college was interesting when you found chicken beaks and toes in the soup, but the flavor was always good. Really our accommodations where very good, we had nice clean comfortable beds. This trip I could do again.

Portugal has a lot of interesting history. We toured places such as where Columbus studied his navigation and where he departed to discover America.

I had one of the greatest shocks of my life in October 1985. Jeff and Crystal decided to move to Minneapolis. I had gotten to depend on Jeff to manage things that I wasn't sure I wanted to go back to doing myself. Jeff had such a good handle on equipment changes. New equipment was coming out with monitor controls and computerized applications that I had no knowledge of. You know "I was just born too early and didn't learn all that stuff." I thought this was the end.

We rented out to other farmers all the land we owned and I made plans for an auction sale, which we held in April 1986.

For some reason, I hadn't notified the landlords of 5,000 acres we were renting. I had all winter to think about a plan and decided to keep farming the rented land. Doug Ely and Terry Ost were with us, so we were able to farm. Neighbors said it didn't make sense to rent out our own land and then rent land back from someone else, but it worked.

Terry was an excellent farm helper. He did a lot of maintenance work and trucking in the wintertime. He could even replace truck motors and repair them.

Doug's job was more with seed and chemical sales. We were getting crop chemicals in bulk delivery. Doug would fill farmers' tanks as they came in. We also sold fertilizer and had a mixing machine to make up certain blends. Mr. Odegard, a retired county agent, came on board to help with fertilizer and chemical applications.

Now the need had come for more spaces to park homes in Bismarck. Harley Swenson and Harold Schultz had acreage on the east side of town, so we joined together and began construction of Century Park with 530 spaces. This was an easy one with the help of good partners.

"A dream takes on a life of its own."

Robert H. Schuller

We always tried to make time for hunting. We need to go back to 1973 when Bob Unterseher surfaced again. I told you these good guys just keep coming back.

It was Bob, Pastor Miller, Si and I who took off for Montana to hunt for elk. Taking horses, we headed for Bob Marshall Wilderness. It was exactly that. Bob found four horses to take along, hauling them in a trailer. The last 20 miles up the mountain was tough going.

We needed the horses to carry our supplies. Things like a tent, a stove to cook on, (no good for heat), water for us and for horses, oats, our sleeping bags and extra clothing, plus food for four days for four guys.

Part of the trail was very dangerous. I could not have ridden the horse had I known the trails on the side of the mountain were only wide enough to walk on with your shoulder against the rock and 1,000 feet straight down on the other side. It had snowed on the trail and some spots thawed and froze. It was slippery. We did a lot of praying to hang on. Twenty miles seemed to take forever. We set up camp on what seemed to be a dry spot. Next morning, it had snowed and it was cold. Oh man! Did you ever try to change clothes inside a sleeping bag? You just kinda feel around under there hoping you have hold of the right thing, no peaking in side. In the warmest part of the day, sitting in the sun, it was still cold!

The first morning of the hunt we stood a little way from our camp hoping a big elk would wonder by. Bob had a long black tube he would blow in which emulated the sound of a bull elk bugling. All we heard in return was birds chirping. We were freezing to death. After what seemed a long time, Bob said, "there, that was a bull elk bulging".

All I heard were the birds. We listened intently. After about ten minutes he said, " there it is again". It was to cold to continue standing there, so we decided Bob and Si would pursue the imaginary bull elk and Pastor Miller and I would proceed up the side of the mountain on the opposite side of the canyon. After about an hour we heard three shots. Bob and Silas shot a six point bull elk. (The head mount hangs in our office today). It was late in the night before we got the elk down off the mountain. We went back to camp and got the horses. They weren't to fond of the smell of the elk. We loaded the elk head, which kept spooking the horse. It went pretty well until we went through some high brush. The horns of the elk rattled the bushes and really spooked the horse. She started bucking and bucking until she threw the elk off into a small stream. This was all at night. Talk about problems trying to load back up in the dark. Bob coined a statement which we tease him about to this very day.

"There is elk all over them hills."

Bob Unterseher

On one of these trips to Montana, Bob and Wesley Loven were together. Bob says, "Wesley, I can get you a free Christmas tree out here in the mountains." So Wesley went out and cut down a nice six-foot pine tree. Bob agreed to haul it back to Jamestown on top of his motor home. The only thing wrong was that the tree came about two months later. Wesley and Judith put up the tree just before Christmas. In bed that night, Judith thought she heard it raining. The outside temperature when they went to bed was well below zero. They got up the next morning and found all the needles of the tree on the floor. All that remained were the decorations on skinny looking branches. That was the end of the Montana tree. The sound of rain was the needles hitting the tinfoil floor covering under the tree. They took all the decorations off, threw it outside and went to town and bought a Christmas tree just like they had done for many years previously.

Twelve
GOD'S SOVEREIGN PROTECTION

MIRACLE 22 Later in the fall, Bob came back to the farm one more time to help move some dirt and to maybe earn a few dollars. Things went well until there was an accident. The following is a true story as written up and published in the Pentecostal Evangel, a worldwide magazine published by the Assemblies of God.

Spare His Life God, Spare His Life

I (Bob) set the earth scraper bit in the soil and heard the RPMs of the powerful diesel engine drop as it began to load dirt. Once the bit was set I never looked back. The drainage ditch I was building required precision. Any glance over my shoulder would create a glitch. The 250-horse power tractor bore down as it filled the bucket with rich, heavy soil. I suddenly felt a tremendous impulse to check the loading scraper. I turned my head for a split second and to my horror, I saw the front wheel of the scraper knock a co-worker to the ground. My feet hit the clutch and the brake at the same time. The tractor stopped abruptly. The front wheel of the scraper was sitting directly on top of a man with the scraper half full of dirt.

It was early October. I called Jon Liechty, a businessman and close friend, to ask if he could use some help for a month. He was building a drainage system on one of his farms south of Jamestown, North Dakota. He could use the help so I committed to 30 days. I had operated heavy equipment for Jon in the past, leveling land for mobile home parks.

There were three of us working on the project that day, Wesley Loven, Jon's brother-in-law, and Kenis Loven, Wesley's son. Wesley was our rod man. His job was to read the depth of the cut area to prevent the ditch from going too deep. If too deep the water would stand, if not deep enough it would be a dam.

I lowered the scraper bit to just a couple of inches above the ground as the tractor closed in on the cut area. Wesley, with the eye level, stood with a long stick pointing at the spot where the bit should begin loading the scraper. The bit touched the earth and the tractor began to lug. That's when I looked behind me and saw the front wheel of the scraper hit Wesley and knock him down to the ground. Thousands of pounds of dirt were sitting on top of him.

I grabbed the hydraulic lever to raise the scraper bit. Thoughts were racing through my mind. If I lift the scraper, all the weight of the dirt will crush him for sure. At full throttle I put the tractor in reverse and slowly let out the clutch. Everything was moving in slow motion. Black smoke billowed out of the exhaust pipe as power was transferred to the wheels. The tractor began to jump up and down under the strain, while the scraper bit broke loose from the earth and slowly moved backward. My training as a certified Emergency Medical Technician, while in a previous pastorate in Colorado, came quickly to mind as I leaped out of the tractor and ran back to where Wesley lay motionless on the ground. The scene was familiar to me. His face was very white indicating a lack of circulation and possible severe internal injuries. He was not breathing and there was no pulse. In my mind, I had just killed my friend.

As I knelt beside Wesley's motionless body, turned my face toward heaven, and in a loud and persistent voice, I cried, "Spare his life, God, spare his life!" I continued to repeat the short prayer until I saw Kenis running from his tractor and scraper to where his father lay on the ground.

"What happened?" he shouted as he ran and fell at his father's side.

"I just ran over your dad. Go get the pickup!" I shouted. "Radio the office. Tell the secretary to call the emergency room and tell them that we are on the way!"

I triaged his chest to see if it was crushed. "We will have to do CPR until medical people arrive?," I asked myself. Just then I thought I heard a slight groan. Listening more closely, yes it was! Wesley's eyelids were twitching like he was trying to open them. Listening even closer, I thought, Wesley is trying to tell me something.

Then, more distinctly I faintly heard him say, " Help me up."

Perplexed and with grave concern I shouted, "Wesley, I just ran over you. You probably have internal injuries. Please lay still. We've got to get you to the emergency room."

"Help me up," he emphatically repeated.

By this time Kenis had returned with the pickup. "Your dad wants to stand up." I told Kenis.

I couldn't believe he was alive, let alone talking and wanting to stand up. It didn't occur to me that we had witnessed a miracle.

I looked at Kenis and said, "Okay, help me get him up."

We reached under his arms and lifted him to his feet. He let out a moan and collapsed to the ground. Picking him up again, we quickly put him into the pickup seat and drove out of the field with Wesley pressed hard against the door. We kept glancing at him to see if he was still breathing, it seemed like I heard Wesley say something.

"What did you say?" I asked.

In slow raspy voice he said, "Take me home."

I was sure I hadn't heard right. "Wesley, I just ran over you with the scraper. You may have internal injuries. You could be bleeding inside. You have to go to the hospital." I explained.

In a more stern voice I heard him say, "Take me home."

By this time his wife, Judith had received a phone call about the accident. She was getting ready to go to town when we pulled into the yard. Wesley was sitting up in the truck. Judith came running out of the house and up to the passenger side of the pickup. Wesley rolled the window down and asked her to bring his walker. He explained he was going to take a shower and put on clean clothes.

Judith brought the walker and he slowly made his way into the house without assistance. We were all astonished when he emerged twenty minutes later looking like a new man.

At the hospital a waiting team of medics wondered what was taking us so long. They were waiting outside at the ER entrance with a gurney when we arrived. They quickly rushed him into the examination room. Judith and I waited for over an hour before the doctor appeared asking to see who had run over this man with the scraper. I slowly stood to my feet and raised my hand. The doctor walked promptly to where I stood and asked me to explain what had happened out in the field. I told him every detail I could remember. When I finished he looked puzzled.

The doctor remarked, "I have examined and x-rayed this man for over an hour and I cannot find anything wrong with him. I am going to keep him in the hospital for a few days for observation to make sure everything is alright." This was truly a miracle.

Amos Stoltsfus had run our harvest crew five years and decided he had had enough. He found us a good replacement with John and Pat Swiers. Their family was just getting to the age where he had good built-in help. Pat was also involved very much. I always said she was the best combine operator they had.

Swiers' harvesting crew ran the combines the next thirteen years. Starting in Oklahoma and working their way back to North Dakota each year. They were good with trucks and equipment and still got a lot done. We had real peace of mind when Pat and John were in charge. We knew things were going well and that we would get our fair share.

It was exciting to watch the family children grow up. Each year you would see new expressions on the faces of the four boys. Some of them changed enough in one year we had to ask them their name again. Then there was Jill, their only girl, she was always witty and ready for a laugh.

Driving combines really made an impression on their boys. When their oldest son, Jessie, decided to get married, an outdoor wedding was held. When we got to the wedding, there stood one

Four of our John Deere combines operated by John & Pat Swiers' crew.

of our combines. When the wedding service was over at the altar, which was right close to the combine, the bride and groom climbed into the combine and used that as their drive away vehicle. What a blast!!

In 1987 we were offered the opportunity to buy the 96 unit Pheasant Run Apartments in Williston. This was an easy project built along side the airport, good access by airplane. Williston oil drilling was in recession and this let us get a good buy on these units.

This was also the year that Bob (here he comes again) took me elk hunting in Colorado. This was a dry run. The weather was too warm, pushing the elk higher up into the mountains. This time we didn't use horses. We walked back into the woods and hills. I remember posting all by myself. I was sitting, watching, when all of a sudden two young elk popped out of nowhere and scared me half to death. I forgot all about shooting.

Another time while driving across Montana with our family and Bob, Bob said, "Let's stop and check out this mountain, we may see some deer." Stopping there, Bob said that Jeff, Sherry and I should go around one way and he would go around the mountain the other way meeting at the other side. Going back in was fine until it started to snow. I lost all sense of direction because the sun had gone behind a cloud. I didn't want Jeff and Sherry to think we were lost, although we were, and I did not know what to do or where to go. Just then Bob showed up, he said he figured we might be lost. That time I was as angry at Bob as I have ever been. But I couldn't stay mad at him for very long because he was our ticket back to the vehicle.

This was also the year our Concord Manufacturing Company decided to put an air seeder in the field in Czechoslovakia. Darryl

Daryl Justeson and I putting a Concord Air Seeder and soil tester in the field in Czechoslovakia.

Justesen and I were asked to go. Terry Mortenson, a missionary to that country, was our interpreter. This was behind the Iron Curtain on a 3,000 acre communist farm. The work went well. We had the machine together and running in three days. We ate our meals in their community mess hall. It was interesting to discover that I farmed more acres in North Dakota with three to five hired hands in contrast to their 3,000 acre communist farm that employed five hundred people. Most of their work was done by hand. They made everything from bread and butter to clothes and tools all by themselves. They raised all their own fruits and vegetables and seemed to have a lot of pride in their wineries. There were lots of grapes and huge tanks of wine. They had very modern equipment in the shop.

Eventually it was time to sell our 172 Cessna which I still miss flying today. We bought into a flying group with three other friends who purchased a six passenger Piper Lance with retractable gear. This is a faster plane and carries a bigger load. One day, with the Piper Lance, I flew Darryl Justesen and Jack Oberlander to Kansas to view a new type seed wagon which my friend Ron Neff, and who's father we had combined wheat for many years in the seventies, had developed. Another time I picked up Howard Dahl, President of Amity, and we flew to South Dakota to the State Fair there. Keith Veil, a part owner in the plane, and I have made numerous trips through Colorado, Kansas, and Nebraska. One time Fern and I and Mike flew to Rockwall, Texas. This is a comfortable fast way to go.

Nineteen eighty-eight was another year of opportunity. The large Freddie Mutschler farm came up for sale. Silas and I bought a total of 2,400 acres giving John Mutschler, a brother of Freddie, an option to buy back 480 acres.

Silas and I had often talked about getting some land in the south to have for our custom harvest run. An ideal number would be a section, 640 acres, of land in each state from North Dakota to Texas.

"Trust in the Lord and do good;
dwell in the land, and feed on his
faithfulness. Delight yourself also in
the Lord and he shall give you the
desires of your heart" (Psalms 37:3-4).

Maybe this was the beginning of our dream. John Mutschler decided to exercise his option. He okayed a trade if we could find land elsewhere. Our friend in Kansas, Adam Nusz, had wanted us to buy land that he could farm in Kansas. Adam had his eye on 480 acres there.

John Mutschler bought those 480 acres and then we traded back with him. That left Silas and I with 1,920 acres of the Mutschler farm. Later Adam Nusz found another 240 acres he wanted to farm nearby in Kansas plus the 480 acres we had traded.

In February of 1989 our brother Paul passed away. Paul was nearest my age of the brothers. Growing up we paired up a lot like this, Adam and Ezra, Jonathan and Paul, then Silas and Reuben.

Paul and I did a lot of things socially together. He was only 18 months younger than I. We were two grades apart in school. Paul was always mature for his age. We went to parties together, roller-skating and ice-skating. We had many double dates with girls, but never married those younger gals. Paul was always eager to drive dads cars, and I didn't care if I drove or not. We hunted skunks and trapped fox. We had a lot of fun. Paul and I did some farming and combining together. We also bought a half section of farmland from Mary Bowman.

Paul went into the ministry about the same time I began farming. Paul was a great evangelist and we tried to support him as much as possible. Being limited in funds in my early days, I remember telling my mother I wish I had enough money to give Paul $100 per month toward his ministry. Seems like a drop in the bucket now.

Paul and I got along well. As time went on Paul began selling cars at Stoudt's Ford dealership in Jamestown. Later Paul opened his own used car sales on main street. I bought cars and pickups from him as he opened his sales lot in Jamestown. But I must confess, I could have done better. Looking back, which is too late now, I wish I had helped him more. The last few years of Paul's life were spent in Texas. Paul and Jean moved to the Dallas area to be closer to their children. Paul had a start of melanoma before he left North Dakota. He spent his last six months in the Houston cancer treatment center.

I have appreciated Jean, Paul's wife, the children, and their hospitality. Some of their boys have come back to North Dakota to hunt with me. This has been a lift to my spirit. I feel it's still part of Paul.

One other sad note this year was the fire of our farm shop. It being December and winter

Jean and Paul Liechty

time we had the 120 X 60 building full of equipment. A new John Deere combine, three tandem grain trucks, two tractors, a Concord Air Seeder, antique Ford tractor, and thousands of dollars of tools all burned up plus the building burned to the ground. Often we wonder why, but never underestimate God's plan.

The year 1989 offered us some apartments in Fargo. Liechty Homes, Liechty Associates, and Reuben Liechty bought a 77 unit complex there.

In January of 1990 Fern and I went on another MAPS trip to Argentina with a church group from Eden Prairie, Minnesota. Fern helped make bed furniture for the dorms. I laid up cement blocks on a three-story college building. These are great times of refreshing, using your talents to help build something for other people, people that have nothing to build with and nowhere to get it. We both thank the LORD for one more opportunity to give back some things we have been blessed with. Rocky and Sherry Grams, Mike and Mona Shields were our hosts.

The year of 1990 was both a good year and a sad year. This was the year the mother of us boys passed away. Mom had lived a full life of 96 years. According to my estimation she was one of the great ladies of all time. There wasn't a selfish bone in her body. Mom was always helping someone. At the age of 90, she was still going to the nursing homes, singing and playing the piano for the older residents there. Her grandchildren spent a lot of Saturday noons with her for lunch. Mom could make, it seemed like, lots of food out of nothing and it was really good. Fried cornmeal mush, baked beans, potato salad, and homemade bread were some of her specialties. Dandelion salad with hard-boiled eggs was another. She made homemade cheese and green peppers filled with sauerkraut.

The most outstanding part of her life was her prayer time. You could count on each day after noon lunch, Mom would go to some corner of the house and pray. We never heard what she said but you can be sure she named all her children and grandchildren many times.

I count it a modern day miracle, when divorce rates are 50%, none of her six children and only two out of twenty-two of her grandchildren ever went through a divorce.

"She keeps a close eye on the conduct of her family,
and she does not eat the bread of idleness. Her children
and her husband stand up and bless her. Many women
have done a noble work, but you have surpassed them
all."(Proverbs 31:27-29)

In the fall of 1990 I had the pleasure of seeing the Grand Canyon of Colorado. As luck would have it, my friend, Bob Unterseher, had a friend, Bruce Akin, who lived at the bottom of the canyon. He worked for the U.S. Government, taking care of a water pumping system for the North Rim resort He had a beautiful three-bedroom home at the bottom of the canyon. Bob had held a children's crusade years before at Grand Canyon Village on the south rim. Bruce brought his children. They had become friends.

We flew to Las Vegas, rented a car and drove to the canyon. It was five miles all down hill to the bottom. We decided to walk down. You better have good shoes and good feet for a hike like that. My feet were very sore from holding back as we went downhill. Bob's knees got very sore, so we finally took off our undershirts and wrapped his knees so he could make it. By the time we reached the bottom, they would no longer bend.

Down in the canyon we took hikes and did some fishing. Our host was an artist and writer. We spent time in his gallery. We were treated royally.

Coming up out of the canyon was yet before us. I tried walking out one mile as a test and decided I could not walk all the five miles up. We rented three mules, one for our luggage and one for each of us. That was a good ride, except the mules didn't walk on the path. They walked on the outside of the trail, near the edge of the cliff, because they normally carried large packs that would rub the rock wall on the inside. We leaned toward the wall as we rode along. It was 1,000 feet straight down. We had sore feet going down and coming out we had sore seats.

I am standing on trail entering the Grand Canyon of Colorado.

Another farm, the 960 Hoggarth farm, came up for sale. This was our first irrigated ground. The farm had two pivots on it. There was plenty of water below. We tried potatoes one year on our own, but we didn't have proper contracts so we went back to cash rent. As of now, we have a man cash renting the ground for potatoes every 2nd or 3rd year. I have been farming the ground in the years in between.

The 90s brought us into a new goal of giving with all we had going. We thought we should try to give 50% of our profits away. I can't tell you how it works, except we know Jesus helped us many times. Sometimes we had normal setbacks, but it was our test and with determination we always came out on top.

"Give and it will be given to you. A good
measure, pressed down, shaken together
and running over, will be poured into your
lap. For with the measure you use, it will
be measured to you" (Luke 6:38).

MIRACLE 23 Before we get moved away from the Montpelier farm I should tell you about our neighbor, Frank. Frank moved in on a section of land right next to our farm. He was a very reserved type of fellow. I watched him farm several years right across the road. Driving past him on a tractor he never would wave or recognize that he ever saw you. I thought the guy must be mad at me. One day I got my tractor stuck across the fence from him. I thought, "This may be my chance to try him out." I walked over and asked if he would pull me out. "Yes," he said. He gave me a pull, wouldn't take any money for it, and this was the beginning of our friendship. We got to be good friends. Frank started coming over to our place to talk farming. Being I was farming more than he, he ask me how I could sleep at night and how I knew where to start each day. In a few years Frank got sick with cancer and ended up in the hospital. I visited him a few times, prayed with him, and led him to the Lord before he died. I was asked to be one of his pallbearers at his funeral.

Thirteen
NEW OPPORTUNITIES FOR BUSINESS AND MINISTRIES

As I stated before in chapter four, two men I have observed for years, I find an interesting and maybe a sad conclusion. Jim and Joe were cousins. Jim you might say was born with a silver spoon in his mouth. Joe on the other hand came from a poor home. His father was an alcoholic. Jim started farming the home place where his dad left off. Joe got started farming by renting a small piece of ground.

Sorry to say Jim died fairly early after middle age. He had lost some of the farm that was handed over to him. Many times I saw Jim go through our little town and stop for a beer which cost him both time and money.

Joe accumulated much farm land and has great holdings of property. The lesson here is, it's not how much you start with, as much, as how you manage what you have. It isn't always good to start a man with money, when he doesn't know where it came from or how it got there.

There were two other tycoon farmers who were interesting to watch, and when I thought I was in a slow pace, trying to hang on, it seemed there was nothing that could stop Bill and Ben. I took a farm tour out to Bills large tractor barn with six big John Deere tractors and equipment. Ben's farm with ten tractors, airplanes, and motor homes, don't know what really happened, these guys just couldn't hang on to all their property and investments. You would have thought they were on top of the world financially.

The nineteen eighties were stressful dry years. Anyone who was over-leveraged at the bank had tough going. Slowly Bill and Ben started selling off their properties, some was foreclosed on until Ben had nothing left and Bill had very little. Sad to say none of these guys ever took time for church and probably never gave much to charities. The Lord wants at least 10% or more.

When we started thinking about moving to town we rented our farmland to Duane Huber. He, along with the Mutschlers were going to farm the ground. Fern and I decided we could just as well live in town to do my style of farming. In December, before going to Florida, we had decided on the house in Jamestown. This large four bedroom home with four baths and three fireplaces had a lot of style. The house was built by the Ramstad-Fode families. Built in 1962, using white brick for some outside trim, it seemed rather ironic that we bought the extra brick they had left over and we used it on our new home which we built on the farm at Montpelier back in 1964. Now we are back enjoying that same white brick décor again on our home in town.

In December, from Florida, we sent a deposit to tie up the deal. Reuben Liechty Realty Co. was arranging the sale.

This home now belonged to Dr. Wahe. He had moved to Texas and had a lady living in the house to keep it heated. The bad part was this lady had two male friends. One got jealous of the other and set the house on fire thinking he would burn up the lovers, but they escaped.

We returned home in February 1991 to see the damage on our new home. It was a total disaster and looked almost impossible to fix up. Fern said she did not want the house. The insurance company said they could make it like new.

Al Leapoldt Construction and Bob Welsh of Service Masters began cleaning and rebuilding. We returned to Florida for another month and returned home late in March. The contractors worked on the house all summer. A lot of new carpet and draperies were installed. The house was completely repainted inside and out. It gave us a chance to install a new larger bathroom. Completely new shingles were put on the roof.

The house was finished and looked much better than when we first decided to buy it. It really was a shame for things to go that way. Someone's loss was our gain.

We made the move from farm to town in October 1991. This was a big move. Moving Fern's collections of forty years of married life was not easy. Backing two trucks into our three-stall garage, we took our time and divided items as we went. Fern's sisters helped with the household items, dividing some in one truck for the house in town, some items went to the other truck to store in the old farm-house until we could have an auction sale. The third part of sorting went to the dumpster. Many months after moving into town, Fern realized some of her best Corning Ware casserole dishes and some other items were missing. When we planned for the auction sale we found they had been put in the wrong boxes.

After we moved to town, we sold the 36-acre farmstead to Mutschlers on contract for deed. With this all in place having rented the farmland to Mutschler-Huber farms we did not need all of our farm equipment. In April 1991 we did our second auction, selling everything except the harvesting combines, trucks and trailers. Another move toward less investment and less responsibility. Later we bought the farm back and resold it to Jay and Diane Schlenker. They are still there today.

New doors opened in 1991 to buy the 96 Carriage House apartments in South Dakota. There were 24 very deluxe units in four different cities, although some units needed some work, they seem to stay full all the time.

A new association had begun in 1991 with Todd Sjostrom,

Our second auction sale of farm equipment.

our friends Lyle and Evelyn's son. Todd came as a helper in the harvest field. He drove combines and trucks. As a college student he was very sharp, yet very polite and easy to work with. Todd had one accident like anyone could have, he rolled over a truckload of wheat on Highway 46. It wasn't speed as much as a top heavy load and there was not much damage on the truck. The wheat was easy to pick up as most of it fell on the black top road. All it took was a grain auger and scoop shovels to clean it up.

I worked Todd into operating our grain elevator and our grain dryer system. He later became elevator manager, routing grain to proper bins, loading and unloading trucks. Along with this, Todd had some sales experience with a paint company. I was the Pioneer Seed dealer for our area. Todd began booking seed orders for me. For that, I paid him on a commission basis. We worked this system for six years. Todd started farming with his dad but kept interested in Pioneer Sales -- more on Todd later.

We were driving out in Washington state visiting friends in 1992, dropping down to Newberg, Oregon to see my Army buddy, Marvin. You heard about him earlier in the book. On our way back up we followed the Columbia River west. The scenery of Columbia Falls and the mountains was beautiful.

MIRACLE 24 This story goes on and on, actually started by taking a neighbor girl, Marilyn Johnson, to Sunday school, written up earlier in this book. We soon turned north up towards Yakima. This was the place where Marilyn and Tim Waddington were living. Actually Tim grew up in this area. Remember, Marilyn was our little Sunday school girl. Tim wanted to show me 80 acres of pasture he wanted to rent to make hay and run a few cows. I went back and talked to Silas and we offered him a 50-50-share crop deal.

Cows on Yakima ranch

This was just the beginning. The next year he found 320 acres we could rent and now we needed 50 cows. This new acreage was alfalfa hay ground. We could irrigate the ground and sell hay to the dairies. This seemed to work well and made jobs for Tim's children who were in their mid-teens. Tim kept going and finding more hay ground for rent. Tim had pushed up acreage to 600 acres and some extra pasture, which needed 150 cows. We were still working on our 50-50-share crop deal.

Back home, some of Bob Reimer's land came up for sale in 1992. This was right beside the Hoggarth farm and seemed like it fit into our mix. We purchased 860 acres.

We bought a small acreage right by the Erickson farm, 250 acres, in 1993. It was so close it connected right in.

This same year we took another MAPS trip to Homestead, Florida. Hurricane Andrew had destroyed a lot of the city, partly taking down the Assembly of God Church and parsonage. We were with a group that included Bob Unterseher (our group leader),

Keith Veil, Joe Beckstrand, Jeannie and Gary Anderson. Also on the job we made new friends with Norvel and Arlene Johnson from York, North Dakota. Fern and Jeannie cooked for the group of workers. We ate good with cooks like that, just one more chance to work for Jesus.

At the end of this same year, Bob Unterseher took us with a group of workers to the Canary Islands where Bruce and Bonita Thomas were the missionaries. This was one of the better MAPS trips we had. The Islands were beautiful, many, many flowers and we found whole sides of hills that had blossomed out with pretty colors. All the colors you can imagine were on sides of buildings and street signs and light poles. The housing where we stayed was several miles from our work site.

They needed someone to drive, who could drive an older stick shift vehicle with steering wheel on the right side. I took the test. The missionaries said they were impressed and I got the job. It was a new experience driving on the left side of the road, especially meeting traffic. My days were filled driving all over the island getting groceries and supplies for 20 some workers. On our return trip we made a stop in Madrid, Spain. Bob had told our Madrid host that people were getting low on cash, so he should get a low priced hotel. The place he picked was on such a narrow street the bus couldn't drive there. We had to carry our luggage one and one half blocks.

Miracle 25 I was entering the hotel that night, on a dark side of the street, two young guys tried to rob me. One came in front, poking fingers in my face while the other guy tried to get my back pockets. I had often thought if I got in trouble I would try to holler real loud to get attention for help. So I did. The guy in back grabbed my left pocket tearing that pocket out and the side seam of my pants, way down to the cuff at the bottom. Bob heard me and saw the young guy, so he grabbed him by the throat and tried to choke him. The young guys broke loose by hitting Bob in the chest with his fist and ran out the door. My credit cards fell out on the floor but the robbers didn't get anything. PTL! We were thankful they didn't have any weapons!

There was very little sleep that night. The staircases were narrow and lighting was poor. People were moving desks and refrigerators in front of the doors of their rooms for fear of break-ins. There was noise on the streets all night long.

No weapon formed against you shall prosper!
(Isaiah 54:17).

Beautiful springtime came in March 1995and we were on our way to Russia and the Ukraine along with a group of Concord's air seeder customers. Among the group going with us were Howard and Ann Dahl, Jerry and Arvilla Peerboom, Ron and Rita St. Croix with their daughter Renee, and several others.

Visiting in the Ukraine we toured a few different farms to look at their styles of farming and the type of equipment they were using and explain the Concord air seeding system.

Among one of these farms we were invited in for a noon meal. The meal was served on a long table that would seat twenty to twenty five people. There was no heat in the building, the temperature out side being about 40 degrees, snow on the ground, it was cold inside at the table. They tried doing their best to keep the food warm but that was hard. They seemed to enjoy lots of Vodka and maybe that kept them warm inside warming up their spirits.

Our ride on a Russian train back to St. Petersburg was a neat experience. We spent two night in sleepers on the train paired up with two couples in each small room. Small beds and no place to hang clothes, bathroom down the hall for the night trips, it got real interesting. We were fortunate enough to pair up with the Peerbooms in our room, they were good sleepers and every one ignored the snoring.

At St. Petersburg we boarded planes back to the US.

Time was moving on and more equipment had accumulated and it was time for another auction sale. The Mobile Home division had acquired lots of things they didn't need anymore. We put it together to make our third auction sale on October 23, 1993.

Sitting on a 4 x 4 x 8 alfalfa bale weighing one ton at Yakima Valley farm.

In 1995 Tim had found a farm for sale in Yakima Valley. It was 170 acres of irrigated hay, plus another 120 acres of Indian ground we could rent. This was the Harry Kwak farm, increasing Tim's acreage up near 900 acres.

It was in the middle 90s when another opportunity opened up in Chicago. A nephew of Silas and Martha, Glenn Mueller,

Cutting cattle by horse on Yakima ranch

More cows added, total of 575 cows

and also son of the late Carl Mueller, wanted financial help on construction of rental buildings. Needless to say this has grown to larger dimensions than was ever thought. Remodeling up to 60 unit apartments and condo buildings. Glenn has done a great job on this and is still continuing to grow. We have had good returns on our investments.

Miracle 26 In 1995 we had a big year at Concord Air Seeders. You remember back in 1985 when Silas and I had arranged money for Concord, some of which we later took in stock. At this time, both John Deere and Case IH wanted to buy our Air Seeder Company. Through Howard Dahl, president of the company, and his good sense of negotiating, the price kept going up. We wound up getting 10 times our investment of stock. It was a pay-off miracle. Silas and I were able to put large amounts of money into a foundation that will give our wives and us a good retirement. After we are gone the money will go to the Church Foundation to help other people.

"Honor the Lord with your wealth, with
the first fruits of all your crops; then your barns
will be filled to overflowing, and your vats will
brim over with new wine" (Proverbs 3:9-10).

I feel the Lord gave me new insight for farming in 1991. As I wrote before, after Jeff left, and Fern and I moved to town, we rented out the land we owned and I kept farming the rented land. We decided to share crop the rented land. We paid more of the cash outlay, my farmer share cropper provided more of the work. We divided seed and fertilizer costs, each of us taking one-half of the crop. This new arrangement let me sell some of our equipment we didn't need. We had a good auction sale, sold some equipment but not the combines and trucks we used in the harvest. We could do some of the harvesting of our crops and also do custom combining, which we have done all our lives. This was our third farm machinery auction.

This also relieved me of need for hired help. The program has been successful and it really took a lot of pressure off me. I had discussed this plan with a good friend and he said he would not want the risk!

"If God can inspire me to believe it,
He can help me to achieve it."

-Robert H. Schuller

One day as I was headed for the field, to check on the men and harvest equipment, I pulled into the gas station for gas. It was the noon hour, but not wanting to stop for lunch I picked up a free bag of popcorn and tried to eat it on the way. I didn't have enough for the guys in the field, so without any water or pop, I tried to choke it down fast before I got to the field. I tried to eat the next morning. I could not get any food down. I began getting a terrible pain in my throat and digestive tract. Fern finally drove me to the emergency room. My throat was plugged all the way down with popcorn. The nurses had to pump out my system. Be sure you drink plenty of liquid when you eat popcorn!

In addition to Doug Ely and Terry Ost, Fred Hoffman came along. Fred was a great man with equipment. He was the only man that had patience enough to drive slowly enough with a disc to eliminate breakage. He was always cheerful and long hours didn't bother him either. I really don't know where he got his drive. Fred was a brother to Rudolph Hoffman, a friend of ours whom we haven't forgotten. Rudolph and Esther visited us, we hunted together at their farm and I served with Rudolph on the church board. We lost Rudolph in a horrible bull accident. That was a real loss to the church and community.

Miracle 27 I must say, during the last five years, with Jeff being gone, the Lord provided the farm with the best of help. It is a blessing to look back and see how He put each one in our path such as Wesley, Henry, Doug, Terry, Fred, Bob, Amos, John, Gerrit, Lyle, Todd, Arthur and others. I appreciated each one of them and with the help of the Lord I can say:

"My help comes from the Lord,
the maker of heaven and earth" (Psalms 121:2).

It was in the middle 90s and we were looking for a ride to Florida. Our friends, Ken and Elsie Wurgler from Minot, offered to take us down. This was a first class ticket in their new Cadillac. It was a fun ride and fast at times. But we took time for some sight-seeing, which included the big arch in St. Louis, Missouri, and also some Ruby caves in Tennessee. Kenny and I had time to discuss the big farm deal. Kenny wore several hats, and one of them, not small by any means, was his farm hat. He and his boys had a good seed business on the farm. With what little I knew, we kept talking farm all the way to Florida.

We arrived at our mobile home park at Dundee, Florida. They stayed with us at our house, and visited back and forth between us and Silas and Martha, who also had a home in our park. We looked around Orlando area at some theme parks and made an attempt at some condos. We got a free breakfast anyway. After the Wurglers left, we only saw them at camp and at some state conventions. We lost Kenny with a heart disease. I had always talked about going up to see their farm but never made it while he was there.

I still had a feeling to go see it, so for three years I went up to either help plant or harvest. Elsie stayed out at the farm with the boys and kept house and cooked. Elsie's meals were wonderful.

On this last page I mentioned our park at Dundee, Florida. Back in 1976, Jon and Silas purchased Dell Lake Village. The park had a clubhouse close to Dell Lake. The park was built to accommodate 250 mobile homes. This was a slow time in Florida. A bank had repossessed the park. There were only 15 homes in place. We thought we had made a fair deal on the park and bought it. It took five years to fill up the spaces. After that, things went along fairly smoothly. Silas and I and our wives each had a home

Fern and Martha Liechty, Elsie and Ken Wurgler

in the park. Fern and I stayed there until the winter of 2007. At this time Bonnie and Lonnie Titus purchased our home in Del Lake Village. Fern and I found a home in Rockwall, Texas close to two of our children and families.

We have had many good times here and have hosted lots of company. Many others have stayed here when we were up home in North Dakota. This area has blessed us, we like it.

Miracle 28 The park in Florida had been an enjoyment in our lives. When we sold the park we put 10% of the money it sold for into the "Donor advised fund with the Assemblies of God Foundation." Each year Silas and I direct income off the funds to many different ministries.

"The only joy of living is the joy of giving."
-Robert Schuller

Remember I wrote about our good friends Howard and Ann

Dahl? Here we are together again. Howard is president of the balance of our Concord company we kept which is now named Amity. Howard and Ann Dahl asked Fern and me to go to Dallas, Texas, to be a guest at a Luis Palau President's Conference. This was a real eye-opener as to the size of his evangelism. To be able to meet such a humble man, one who talks to everybody, and to meet some of the great financial men of the country was a wonderful thing. We met David Hall, owner of the Phoenix Suns, Fred Sewell, owner of a large gas and oil company, Norman Miller, the owner of the Interstate Battery company, Jay Bennett a lawyer with large real estate holdings in Minneapolis, Howard Dahl, manufacturer of sugar beet equipment with sales in Europe and Russia; Wayne Huizenga, with large holdings all over Florida; Dan Konell, national football player, Sean Stepeltong, famous ball player and Stephen Tchividjian, nephew of Billy Graham. These are the kind of people supporting Luis Palau.

We had the privilege in 1996 of financially helping a lady. Her husband left her with three school age children. Debbie was a good mother who worked hard. She always had a job but that didn't cover the expense of bringing up a family. She also fell behind on some medical bills. We gave her enough to buy their groceries for over one year, and have helped periodically since.

"He that knoweth to do good and doeth it
not, to him it is sin" (James 4:17).

THIS MIRACLE BEGIN BACK ON PAGE 140 In 1997 Tim Waddington was calling again, another 150 acre farm came up for sale. This place had two extra mobile homes for housing. He needed a place for his growing family to live. There was also a large shop building he could use for repairing and storing equipment. The farm was all seeded down to alfalfa hay, a perfect fit for what we were doing there.

This put the Waddington's operation, along with more rented land, up to over 1,200 acres of irrigated hay, corn and wheat. Also the cow herd had been increasing to 300 or more and now the final total of cows is 500 head.

This is the type of miracle that has developed just by taking a little young girl to Sunday school. What the Lord started 30 years ago, He planned it right. We have been sharecropping, reaping the benefit all this time.

Marilyn and Tim Waddington 25th Wedding Anniversary

Tim never forgot his calling to serve the Lord. He does a lot of weekend ministry and singing. They are a great Christian family, along with us, believes what Jesus said:

"Seek first the kingdom of God and His
righteousness, and all these things
shall be added unto you" (Matthew 6:23).

Another opportunity came from the Waddington operation to help Case and Karla Vandenberg. They were customers buying our hay for their dairy. Case was a hard working Dutchman from Holland. They were milking cows and needed more cows to fill their dairy barn. Without more credit at the bank, where could they go? Tim Waddington sent them to us. Silas and I bought 80 choice cows for him at $1,000 each on a three-year pay back plan. Case never missed a payment, and he paid us with good interest. When they came to us again, we bought more cows for them. Through the witness of Tim and Marilyn, and maybe ours, Case and Karla started going to church.

Later we got to take an interesting trip to Hong Kong with Luis Palau in 1997. Luis went over for a citywide crusade just ahead of the time when Hong Kong would fall back into the hands of China.

Hong Kong had been under the control of the British until this time. We were asked to go along as prayer partners and help distribute advertising in the city. This was a very modern, busy place. Most all of the American vendors were there, everything from Kentucky Fried Chicken to McDonald's hamburgers. There were also very nice American clothing stores.

Luis held the crusade in a large 40,000-seat arena, which had a roof that could be opened or closed. Large crowds attended and completely filled the arena on the last Sunday. Many decisions for Christ were made.

"The Lord is my light and my salvation
Whom shall I fear?
The Lord is the stronghold of my life
of whom shall I be afraid?" (Psalm 27:1).

From Hong Kong, Fern and I left the party and flew to Tokyo, Japan. A missionary couple met us at the airport and escorted us for three days. We had never seen so many people in all of our lives. We rode the city transit systems, every stop just jammed full of people, both men and women in black apparel. Ladies wore black skirts, white blouses with small black ties and the men wore white shirts, black ties and black coats. With their black hair it was a beautiful sight. We stood on the trains looking down at several hundred people going to work and never have I seen anything more matched looking. It was like seeing a flock of sheep. They all looked alike.

I must say it was hard to find food that we liked. Had it not been for our missionary friend we would have been in big trouble. A lot of their diet comes from the sea. They fix it so differently and some was eaten raw. Our systems couldn't digest it.

The scenery was great. We didn't realize Japan was quite mountainous. Because land is very scarce, the Japanese don't waste one square inch of ground. Either the earth is covered with buildings and streets, or is growing usable vegetation, hillsides and all. The country as a whole was very clean.

> "When I consider your heavens, the work of Your fingers, the moon and the stars, which You have ordained, what is man that You are mindful of him. You have made him to have dominion over the works of Your hands. How excellent is Your name in all the earth!" (Psalms 8:3-9)

MIRACLE 29 Earlier I told you about Todd Sjostrom and me selling seed and working together. In 1997 Pioneer decided to make computers a mandatory part of seed sales. I was born too early, didn't grow up with computers and this really spooked me out of business.

> "Don't give up on the brink of a miracle.
> God's power makes His possibilities achievable!"
>
> -Robert Schuller

Sales award for making the Winners Circle.

This is exactly what happened. Todd had been selling for me on a commission basis. Pioneer agreed to let us do a flip-flop. Todd would be the dealer and I could sell under him. This was an absolute miracle. Normally I would have had to quit business. This was just at the turning point of soybean farming coming into our area. No one would have dreamed how large the soybean sales would become.

At my age, 71, this was an easier way for me. I just needed to book orders and Todd had all the responsibility with Pioneer. The size of sales grew from soybean sales to where I am making three to four times as much money now as before. I would have missed this miracle without it.

Along with our business and farming we have enjoyed an unbelievable social relationship with Todd and Jolene.

They were married August 7, 1993. On January 25, 1999 Noah was born. We have been included in Noah's birthday parties and other family gatherings of the Sjostroms. We were invited to be alongside Noah at his baptism. We are praying that Noah will overcome his infirmity and grow up to be a fine young man. We love him.

Todd, Jolene and Noah have been guests of ours for a week in Florida each of the last five years. We give Lyle and Evelyn a bad

Todd, Jolene, Noah & Belle Sjostrom, July 2007

time by claiming Noah as our grandchild.

We had a great surprise in 1998 when Mom and I became Grandpa and Grandma again. Jeff and Cris had been foster parents to little Jackie. At the age of two, they decided to adopt her. Jackie is just a bundle of joy. We love her.

Fourteen
NEW LEADERSHIP

MIRACLE 30 Nineteen ninety-eight was also the beginning of a new thrust in our family operation. Jeff called one day, after being on his own for 15 years, and asked if he could join our operation. It was the right timing for Dad. I was now in my 70's, wanting to give up some responsibilities. What do you know, we got our son back home! I was one happy father waiting several years for this to happen.

"For the eyes of the Lord go back and forth
throughout the land to strengthen those
whose hearts are fully committed to Him!"
(2 Chronicles 16:9).

Now with Jeff back working with us, we began to look for expansion in various areas. Like I said before, I was looking for farms from North Dakota to Texas.

In the High Plains Journal, a farm was advertised in New Mexico, just three miles from the Texas border. I wondered if this was my Texas answer. With Jeff living in Dallas, he could go check it out. He did all the legwork. Being a pilot, Jeff could look at different farms in short order. He drew up working agreements with the seller and found a good renter to farm the ground. After Jeff had everything in place, Silas and I went down for the closing. This was an 800 acre irrigated farm with 5 pivets on it.

From here on out Jeff had pretty much control of dealing with renting out our own properties. There are a total of 15 different farmland renters to deal with.

Like I said, I continued renting other people's land and farming that, some of it on a share crop basis. When dealing with share croppers, there are right and wrong decisions to make. Sometimes it may seem that two different ways are both right. I was working out a crop insurance report and wondering whose answer was right. That very night as I turned to Proverbs for devotional reading I got my answer and made my decision. "Dishonest scales are disgusting to the Lord, but accurate weights are his delight" (Proverbs 11:1).

Super corn crop on New Mexico irrigated farm.

With Jeffrey being on board, living in Texas, he had his eye out for business opportunities in his area. He got us hooked up with local contractors at White Bluff, Texas. This is a large 4,000-lot ranch that has been subdivided for building homes. This development has a hotel, swimming pools and golf courses. Our part of this project is to provide spec homes to be sold. We keep one or two homes up for sale, the contractor builds the home, and after the sale we divide the profits with the builder. This has been an interesting thing to watch. We thank the Lord for another good connection.

MIRACLE 31 In 1999 a new opportunity opened up for us for manufactured home sales in another city. One hundred forty acres up against the south side of Minot was offered to us. It was still considered farmland and was bought for that kind of price.

Curtis had taken Silas' position in the home sales division a few years prior to this time. Now we see a new team of managers and directors. Jeff and Curtis have now taken over and put Silas and me on the board of directors. It has amazed me how well Curtis and Jeff can work together. It has blessed me to no end.

The next year, after buying the land at Minot, we put in a sales office and began construction of Prairie Bluff for manufactured housing, which included building 62 spaces. This is one more miracle. We already have corporations wanting to buy part of this property.

"God doesn't say "No." He does say "Grow!"
-Robert Schuller

He that soweth sparingly shall also reap sparingly,
He that soweth bountifully shall also reap
Bountifully,
Every man according as he purposeth in his heart,
so let him give;
Not grudgingly, or of necessity: for God loveth
a cheerful giver.   (2 Corinthians 9: 6-7).

By this time, John Swiers' family was all grown into adulthood. Jessie and Justin were both married and had children of their own. They just couldn't make the combine run down south. Then the best driver and stabilizer, Pat, underwent back surgery.

It was time to reduce the harvest fleet from four units down to two. Jon and Silas had a farm equipment auction sale a FOURTH time. We sold off two combines, extra trucks, trailers and miscellaneous equipment. This was a successful sale.

Back in 1994 we organized Dakota Custom Harvesters. This included Reuben Liechty and Reg Herman. Back to the concept of connections, it was true again. The whole thing fell together as another added blessing from above. It just seemed the more we grew and gave away, the more good people the Lord put in our path. Reg and Reuben are both square shooters and are a pleasure to do business with. Reuben, Silas and I have farmed together, bought apartments and real estate together. Like Jack Wilkenson said, "surprisingly enough, we are still friends."

In Dakota Harvesters we had a powerful trading group. It was big enough that we could afford to buy new combines every year, trading up to nine new machines a year, at reduced prices.

Now that John Swiers had resigned his position, here came a call from our farmer, Adam Nusz, asking if he could run our harvest machines. It fit right into our circle. Remember the story of Adam and Arlene who sat in the truck during a rainstorm? Arlene came along to drive truck. She was a good driver! Along with them they brought another connection, Jamie Beachy, who would take on the operation the next year.

MIRACLE 32 Our next farming attempt was in Minnesota. We purchased 970 acres with six irrigation pivots on it. There being a lot of water, it looked like a good farm to buy. We were able to pick up some added blessings on this farm. Normally on irrigation pivots there are corners on every field that don't get water, which leaves those areas as non-profitable. We were able to get a CRP contract on the corners making a payment each year. Also another offer came from a Minneapolis firm wanting to put up wind towers to generate electricity. We have had three towers put up with hope of getting three more. The income from those two plums will pay more than half the interest costs on the farm.

One day while driving around in Bismarck, North Dakota I met with my nephew, David Sjostrom, who was asked by the North Dakota District Council of the Assemblies of God to start a new church. David was one of the college kids who worked for me five summers back in the 70s on the farm.

David graduated from Northwest College, married Connie Nickell and they began ministry as youth pastors in Washington. Later they moved to North Dakota and took the position as youth and children's pastor in our church in Jamestown. We have always kept in contact with Connie and Dave. Bob and Sharon Unterseher came on staff with Pastor Leo Miller to serve as our children's pastor two years before the Sjostroms joined the church staff. That started a community contact program and bus ministry. The program grew to where we had four buses picking up kids every Sunday morning. David took the buses out to our farm shop at Montpelier, sanded and painted them a hot pink. Eileen Miller put her hand to painting Snoopy and other cartoon figures over the hot pink paint. Eileen did a great job. Even the city used our buses a few times.

MIRACLE 33 Back to our drive in Bismarck, Dave was showing me some possible sights where they might build a church. The property they were looking at was way out in the far edge of town with no good accessibility. I drove him by a new piece of property we had acquired for placing manufactured housing. Our two parks, one of 400 spaces and the other of 530 spaces, were almost full, so we needed to look for more land. We bought 40 acres on the north side along a busy main road into Bismarck. One corner along the road was zoned commercial and would make a good spot in a residential area for the new church.

Capital Christian Center, Bismark

That was exactly what happened. Connie's Dad, Gordon Nickell, who had moved to Bismarck, was an architect and had drawn many church plans.

It's thrilling to see how the Lord can put things together, like Pastor Dave, architect Gordon and us as property owners.

Now stands the new large Capital Christian church facility that will include an educational department. Dave says the Lord had us buy that property just so he could build His church. He also moved Gordon to Bismarck just for that.

Our blessing was the fact that we got some tax relief for the gift.

"The mind of man plans his ways.

But the Lord directs his steps!" (Proverbs 16:9).

⇒ *Fifteen* ⇐
FERN'S COOKIES

I must break in here and say that ever since we purchased the mobile home park in Dundee, Florida back in 1975, Fern and I have had the privilege of spending three months in Florida each winter. That is, if certain goals were met before it was time to go. I am referring to Fern's cookie baking.

Day one is spent searching through all kinds of recipe books, as many as 50 books, trying to decide which kinds and how many of each different kind of cookies and some candies she finally will decide to make.

Day two we start assembling a lengthy list of needed supplies. The next step is to head for at least three grocery stores to be able to complete the proper needs and brand names, which is most important for quality taste. Now this list of groceries includes:

Coconut
Chocolate chips
Butterscotch chips
Almond bark-white
Almond bark-chocolate
Nuts – all kinds
Candy sprinkles
Candied fruit
Dates
Raisins
Eagle brand milk
Eggs
Cream
White sugar

Brown sugar
Powdered sugar
Flour

By the end of the third day with little conversation, pulling into the garage with the town and country van, I hear the first request as we get into action. "Jon, would you please unload the groceries for me? I am tired and cold and it's snowing outside." After several trips to the garage and back, unloading, I hear a request, "Could we go out and find something quick to eat? I want to start baking tonight." Around 11 o'clock I go to bed while candy is being stirred and the oven is roaring. I wake up at 1:30 and there I am still alone in bed.

The next day, day four, brings out stacks of cookie sheets, cake and candy pans and knives plus the giant mixing machine and two hand-held mixers. At this point the kitchen sink and four burner stove have completely diminished out of sight. Now the kitchen

Fern's Cookie Baking Sheets

table is becoming the victim of tablecloths of various shapes and colors. After 12 hours of this I again fall into a king size bed. I awaken at 2:30 and still no sight of a bed partner.

Entering the fifth day we have come to the climax. Now it's time to prepare for the cookie tray wrapping. This cannot start until all baking dishes are scrubbed and returned to their proper places. This being church night, it was the annual Christmas party and cookie tasting night. It was a chance to exhibit two of the largest trays of cookies in the house. After completing the ladies baking competition, we go home only to start wrapping cookie trays. It is now 11:30 P.M. I am involved in the process, finally running out of trays at 1:30 in the morning.

Day six, we buy more trays so that after work we can finish the job. Now I forgot we had supper engagements with friends in Valley City, 35 miles away. This delayed the cookie tray wrapping again until 11:30 P.M. We finished the job at 1:30 A.M.— a total of 32 trays.

Fern's cookie trays ready to deliver to her friends.

Fern had put together two Christmas presents for me to open that night after cookie tray wrapping. Having been up late two nights wrapping cookies, I was in no shape to open presents. I was more disgusted on the inside than what appeared on the outside. Anyway, I didn't show much appreciation for a book I didn't care for and a game I knew nothing about. I did however repent and ask for forgiveness. This was the beginning of Christmas.

Now I must say that although I did drag my feet on some of this project, the returns of cards of thanks and praise that Fern got for all her efforts was well worth the labor. Now it came time to deliver cookies to 32 homes. Again, I was not too excited about this part of the process. Although I agreed to drive the car, I was reluctant to go to the doors with some of the cookie plates. At one of the homes, Fern went to the door. There were no handrails, the steps were icy, the dog jumped up and barked. Fern started sliding backwards, landing flat on her back in a snow bank, holding the cookie tray right side up, not spilling a cookie she said, " I saved the cookies!" It did, however, hurt her back. This was the night before we left for Florida. To say the least, I went to the doors after that fall. Arriving in Florida, Fern went to the clinic for x-rays and treatment.

I must tell you about my friend, Jim Vandrovec. We had met a few times before. Jim stopped by, wondered if I had time to pray. I was working out in the yard and we stopped right there and had a prayer meeting. This was the beginning of our continued friendship. We have golfed together many times. One summer we flew to Dallas and played golf with Jeff in a tournament at Jeff's church. Jim has included me in his golf committee for Youth for Christ fundraiser. Most times we meet for coffee one half hour before church. Jim will stop at our house at random most any time. One time he brought over a video for us to watch with him. It wasn't long till he was lying on the floor sleeping and then I would be sleeping also. Fern wanted to bring us coffee but that didn't help. We have had many Bible discussions and have passed out religious tracts. Jim is a real cut-up type person, he likes to joke around and make people laugh. When I was recovering from open-heart surgery, he came to visit me in the hospital. When I got out of bed to go to the bathroom, Jim crawled into my bed and got under the covers. A nurse came in and almost flipped. She thought she was in the wrong room.

Darrel Losing, Jim Vandrovic, Jim Exner, Jon Liechty
Youth for Christ has been a big part of Jim and my activities.

Sixteen
GOD'S HEALING TOUCH

In April of 2001, I brought shocking news to everyone. We had just returned home from Florida. It was my first day out to the farm. I was repairing a truck tarp and up on a ladder stretching over the side as far as possible. I got a pain in my right arm. I knew it wasn't an ordinary pain.

Having some loose parts to take to town for repair, I took them in to Midwestern Machine, owned by my friend, Keith Veil, to get fixed up and the pain in my arm continued to grow. I had planned to stop in town for lunch. By this time I was really hurting and decided to head for home.

I called Fern and said I'd be home for lunch. Fern had lunch ready. I ate and said I would sit down and rest. I had no sooner sat down when the pain started traveling up my neck. I called Fern, "Get me to the emergency room as soon as possible!"

I didn't know why she needed to change clothes. Why didn't she drive faster? "Don't stop at that stop sign. Let's go!" I was in desperate pain.

As soon as I arrived, they had me lie down, clothes and all and put nitroglycerin tablets under my tongue. This definitely cut down the pain. After Dr. Johnson's diagnosis, he said, "you were trying to have a heart attack." I responded, "I'm not trying very hard." Dr. Johnson said I definitely had heart blockage. They placed me in an ambulance and took me to Bismarck Med Center One Hospital.

I arrived on Friday evening. Since the doctors were gone for the weekend, they just kept me in bed and stabilized me until Monday when they ran tests. Wednesday, April 25 2001, they prepared me for open-heart surgery.

About now is when I began to have sobering thoughts, especially when the doctor came in and had me sign a paper releasing him from liability in case I died. I must say that in and through these thoughts I had perfect peace. Some people say they think of things they wish they had done. Well, I didn't have any of this. My slate must have been clear. Thank the Lord.

By this time, our daughters Sherry and Jeania had both flown in to be with Mom during the surgery. The nurses were terrific. They must have given me something to put me out. I don't even remember leaving the room on the way to surgery.

The doctor would come out periodically and tell Mom and the girls how I was doing, like, "we've got his heart out," "he is running on a machine," and "doing fine," "now we've put his heart back in and it started." I guess the worst thing for them was when they saw me come out of surgery, all the tubes hooked up all over, three in my stomach, two down my throat and one in my nose. They tell me this is when Mom and the girls lost it.

I came out of the four-by-pass surgery just fine. The nurses started walking me the second day. I was doing so well that in three days I could take my own shower. By Sunday, the 5th day, I was on my way home.

The flowers, cards and visitors were wonderful. The support of our two daughters flying in, Jeania from Dallas and Sherry from Seattle, was so reassuring of great family ties. Even my doctor back in Jamestown, Dr. Johnson, stopped to see me while in the Bismarck hospital. It is great to have friends at a time like this.

My recovery time at home was six weeks and then I began to do small jobs and drive the pickup. I still wanted to farm. I had paid cash rent on many acres, so it wasn't easy to drop all of that.

I just decided that:

"They that wait upon the Lord will renew their strength. They will soar on wings as eagles; they will run and not grow weary, they will walk and not be faint" (Isaiah 40:31).

This was so reassuring to me. The love of God was a firm foundation. I had a chance to have an artist come and carve a wooden eagle out of a tree in our front yard. Our eagle carries the above Scripture verse on it.

My recovery went real well. Looking back, except for the healing power of Jesus—"By His stripes we are healed," it could have been like this inscription I read on a tombstone.

"I used to be where you are
Soon you will be where I am
Are you prepared to join me?"

In recovery these words came to me:
We came down life's road
On kind of an easy way.
Each day gathering a heavier load
Thinking forever we would stay.

All of a sudden
On an ordinary day,
Life faltered, it halted
In an unusual way.

Pain persisted to twist my arm
And up my neck it did ride.
I knew someone had set the alarm
To the doctor I went—Fern as my guide.

This summer will end
The third quarter of life's game.
(on this side of death)
We'll play the fourth quarter
Holding on to Jesus' name.

Thankful for the second chance,
So when He calls again
We will know we won the game.

We know that Jesus will
Add to life its length.
Psalm 118:14 says "He is my strength."

Although I was restricted to 10 pounds to lift, I was still able to keep my farming together. Some was the sharecropping I talked about earlier and I had an opportunity to rent more ground of my own. Altogether I had crop on 4,820 acres.

Because of my recovery period, I decided to lean heavily on Fred and Rick Mutschler to do seeding and spraying. I went into a rental basis with Fred for harvest time. We did get everything done in good time and the year turned out profitable.

Seventeen
ADDITIONAL CONNECTIONS

Fern and I thank the Lord that after surgery recovery, 2002 went on pretty normal. We were back to taking trips. We were able to go to Seattle for a Luis Palau festival. There were huge crowds of up to 100,000 people. Having been to several of the Palau President's conferences we were able to go into the VIP tent. That is where the heart of the whole festival is located. You meet some of the greatest people in the world.

We also have been able to get to Florida each winter for three-month periods. After we sold our park in Florida, we kept a home in the park. This has been a good retreat for us each winter. We have had many, many visitors at this home. With this home we have been able to bless other people needing a break. People like the Bruce Martins from Canada, John Wilkersons, Lonnie Tituses, David and Larry Sjostroms, Bob Untersehers, Adam, Ezra, Silas and Reuben Liechtys, Lowell Lundstrom, Allen Schlenkers, Harvey Wolffs, Elsie Wurgler and her boys, and maybe a few more.

Also we have put the house on the Bid and Dine auction for the Jamestown College fundraiser, that people could rent for a week of vacation and the rent money would go to the college just trying to help people.

Also included in our Florida winters is time spent at Siesta Key Beach in Sarasota. Our children like to meet us there during Christmas and New Years.

We have time-share units there, enough to entertain everyone besides some extra visitors like Duchscherers, Wurglers, and Sjostroms. This is a place right on the beach with a hot tub and pool alongside. We do have one of our annual business meetings there each winter. This is a beach with the most beautiful white sands in the world.

"The best and most beautiful things in the
world cannot be seen or even touched—
they must be felt with the heart." -Helen Keller

The year 2002 was just busier than ever. This was a year when money didn't seem to stop long enough to know we had the stuff around. We had finally reached a new plateau in our charitable contributions. Now we were supporting 50 different people on a monthly basis, places including missionaries, colleges, and our local church and civic affairs, giving up to and sometimes over 50% of our profits.

"Bring ye all the tithes into the storehouse,
that there may be meat in my house, and
prove me now herewith, saith the Lord of
hosts, if I will not open the windows of
heaven, and pour you out a blessing that
there shall not be room to receive it. And I
will rebuke the devourer for your sakes and he
shall not destroy the fruits of your ground
                    (Malachi 3:10-11).

This was the year our harvest friend, Jamie Beachy, who had been here two years before with Adam Nusz, called and asked if he could take over the harvest operation. This was such a blessing and reassurance of good harvest help. It's another connection that keeps coming and coming. We are now going into the third year with Jamie, his brothers and cousins.

"Always look at what you have left.
Never look at what you have lost." -Robert Schuller

Jamie Beachy, his brother Denis and cousin Jarel Yoder from Wolford, ND.

This winter Fern and I could slip out of Florida and visit friends in Arizona. Ez and Marguerite hosted us as we visited various places in Phoenix. Lyle and Evelyn Sjostrom entertained us at their place for two delicious steak dinners. Walter and Hattie Piehl treated our group to a big steak fry.

We spent several evenings playing Skip-bo, a card game, at Ez Liechty's with coffee and pie to follow. The Exners joined us for most of the activities. Jim and Carolyn stopped in Phoenix on one of their around the nation tours. We got to join the LaMoure county group for breakfast, seeing people that Fern had grown up with and gone to school with in Kulm.

We also got to see where Gail Nokelby lives. Gail's mother had just passed away that week and the funeral was the day before we arrived. We toured her home and then took Gail to the Organ Pizza Palace for lunch. Not knowing they would be there, we met up with Ezra and Marguerite and Walter and Hattie Piehl. There were no dull moments in Phoenix. It was a lively 10 days.

The year 2003 opened avenues to put our money where our

Playing Skip-bo with Exners at Ez & Marguerite home in Phoenix, AZ.

mouth is. There were several hurting people that needed help to get over a hurdle.

"Jesus himself said, "It is more blessed
to give than to receive." (Acts 20:35)

We had the opportunity of making five digit loans to the following people.

A construction company friend.

A main street business man.

A friend with a surgical operation.

A friend with church construction.

A friend with huge medical problems.

These were all with no security, and no interest was charged.

This was also the year a young farmer came to us for help. This man became liable for a half million dollars for which he was not at fault. The courts gave him a bad rap. Because of this, the man lost his credibility at local banks. We put up loans to help him, giving him money enough to farm for the next two years.

"He that knoweth to do good

and doeth it not to him it is sin"
(James 4:17).

We had three exciting trips this year including one to Yakima Valley for our annual family business meeting. Tim and Marilyn Waddington hosted us as we toured our farm operation. We also went to the Case and Carla Vandenberg dairy, saw the milking operation going around the clock 24/7. The Valley was beautiful with it's fruit and vegetable farms. Before leaving the Valley, Tim and Marilyn put up a big steak fry, done western style. Real nice! Leaving the Valley we drove to Seattle and were entertained by Bill and Sherry with grilled salmon, nothing lacking there. It was great! Bill and Sherry escorted us up to Vancouver, Canada, to see the beautiful Butchart Gardens of Victoria. We departed from Bill and Sherry with tastes of lots of good food in our mouth.

Howard and Ann Dahl and the Amity Company hosted our second trip. This was an agricultural trip to Moscow, Russia. Amity is the leading manufacturer of sugar beet machines working around the Black Sea area. We went to see them work as well as make new contacts for more sales. We were on farms as large as 25,000 acres. One of these farms had 25 Amity sugar beet lifting machines. Some of these farms owned their own sugar factories. With cheap labor they made sugar very competitive for the U.S. We saw huge piles of raw sugar beets rotting away, all moldy and smelly, waiting to be processed into sugar.

DAHL RECEIVES AWARDS

Howard Dahl, owner of Amity Technology LLC
In Fargo, has been named the SBA's 2006
Region VIII and North Dakota Small Business
Exporter of the Year.

This annual award recognizes business owners, engaged in exporting, who exemplify the entrepreneurial spirit. The Chamber of Commerce of Fargo Moorhead nominated Dahl for the award. Dahl was selected after a statewide and region-wide competition. SBA's Region VIII consists of Colorado, Montana, South Dakota, Utah, Wyoming, and North Dakota Founded in 1996, Amity Technology manufactures sugar beet equipment. We are proud of our leader, Howard Dahl.

Moscow is a modern city, very busy with too many small cars. On six lane streets they would get as much as eight lanes of traffic. Sometimes to pass another car, they drove up on the sidewalk.

From Moscow we flew down toward the Black Sea and toured back by car visiting farms and sugar factories on the way. We got to stay at one of the early Russian Czar palaces for dinner and overnight. Dinner was very good. They served beef, chicken and fresh vegetables. There were several toasts of alcohol to a variety of things. My trip to the edge of the boat, out in the Atlantic, was still fresh on my mind. I had no problem refusing their liquor. This Palace was still maintained by a huge farm conglomerate out of Moscow. This company furnished our cars and drivers all the way up to Moscow, 700 miles.

We were all ready to give thanks to our Lord for having arrived safely. Our drivers drove as fast as the cars would go. Our speed was 100 to 120 mph. They were stopped four times for speeding. They would just bribe the policeman and get in and go full speed again. They never were issued a ticket. Roads were bad too, causing us to hit the ceiling with our heads.

We did get a good tour of Moscow. We had an American guide who lived there named Lynn Weltz. She was a very sweet girl, a North Dakota girl, who was working for Campus Crusade and knew her way around Moscow. We got into the Kremlin and Red Square and other points of interest. There was so much poverty. People dressed poorly and there were lots of sick people. Crime was going on all the time. There was a great lack of churches and Christian atmosphere. We thank Howard and Ann for being such great hosts and for the wonderful trip.

Lynn Weltz, our Moscow guide.

Our third trip was to Dallas for Jeania's wedding November 8th, 2003. I remember earlier, when Larrie wanted to take me golfing, he had something else on his mind. After we finished the game he popped the question, "can I marry your daughter, Jeania"? After he beat me in golf I told him I would think about it. I let him sweat it out. What a great celebration as Jeania took

Larrie Lambeth to be her wedded husband. Beautiful gowns and flowers and a reception that just wouldn't quit. The bride and groom left the wedding in a long black limo. Where they switched vehicles we will never know, but they came back to the reception on a motorcycle in the long brides dress and all.

People attending the wedding came from Detroit, Minneapolis, and Dorothy and Perry Roorda from North Dakota, plus a host of people from the Rockwall and Dallas area. Jeania did well and we have a wonderful new son-in-law. My brothers, 35 years before this, were wrong. They said I would never get to see Jeania graduate from school, here I got to walk her down the aisle at her wedding.

Perry and Dorothy Roorda at our home in Florida.

It was time to buy another farm in Texas, 635 irrigated acres in one section, complete with four pivots, wells, pumps and motors. This farm was just put together three years prior to our purchase and had good modern equipment on it. Another good feature was the fact that Harold Meyers, our farmer in New Mexico, wanted to farm this place also. Harold is a super individual, a good farmer and always pays on time. This was another one of those great connections the Lord put in our life.

And of course, Jamie Beachy was back to begin our harvest in South Dakota and working his way through the wheat harvest, up to the Canadian border, and then returning to harvest our soybeans and corn, finishing the day before it snowed.

This was our biggest year of farming for Silas and me. Along with the 4,820 acres I had the previous year, I was able to rent the John Mutschler farm of 1,300 acres. It was a good year because of soybean prices, even though we got hailed out on the DeLair farm and dried out on the Klose farm. We sold soybeans all the way up from $5.10 to $9.17 per bushel.

Field of our soybeans yielding 53 bushels/acre.

Now it was time again for the Homes division to expand in manufactured home sales. A sales company in Rapid City, South

Dakota and Gillette, Wyoming wanted to sell out. Curt, Bob and Kent negotiated a deal that looked reasonable. This gave us five retail outlets in three states.

"Thus far has the Lord helped us" (1 Samuel 7:12).

"It is no secret what God can do.
What he's done for others, he will
do for you."

We continued our annual trip to Florida leaving December 14, 2003. We arrived in Orlando, stopping a few days at Dell Lake Village in Dundee, then continued on to Sea Club V in Sarasota December 20th, to enjoy our time-shares with all of our family for the next three weeks.

We also conducted a family semi-annual business meeting. While all the children are there, it makes it convenient for meetings.

After New Years, and after several Sarasota cousins' (of which there are many, we've had as high as forty at one time) breakfasts we returned to Dundee, our winter home for the past 25 years.

February 2004 was a busy month. First we attended the Book

Our alfalfa hay baled and stacked ready to be sold.

Governor Hoeven and Jon at wind generator meeting in Fargo.

of Hope meeting at Ft. Lauderdale. On the way, we drove to Miami for Sunday to be with Rich and Robyn Wilkerson, and also the John Wilkersons who have stayed at our place in Dundee two different summers. What a great ministry is going on in Miami. We toured their new sanctuary and office complex. It is unbelievable what the Lord has provided. Monday we drove up to the Book of Hope meeting. Book of Hope Ministries distributes children's Bibles in schools all over the world. They have put out millions of copies. The Lord has provided enough funds that we were able to help and support this ministry on a monthly basis.

After that, we flew back to Fargo, North Dakota, to attend a wind energy tower conference. We would like to put up more windmills on our Minnesota farm. We were privileged to visit with Governor Hoeven and others. Jeff met us there and did an inventory on grass seed in Minnesota. Then we went to Jamestown to wrap up taxes and farm sign-ups.

We just got back to Florida in time to attend a Luis Palau President's conference. These are the highlights of the year. Updates are given and future events are presented, which are real inspiring. Luis' Bible teachings are tops around the world.

March of 2004 went fast, with four trips to Sarasota, playing a few rounds of golf and on March 24th back to North Dakota. Spring was soon to open up. We did get the wheat seeded in April. May turned wet and it rained for three weeks. We couldn't plant any corn or soybeans till the end of May. We were seeding until the middle of June.

On the 25th of June we started for Minneapolis for our family business meeting. After the meeting July 1st we took off to visit our friends in Pennsylvania. We went up over the top of Lake Michigan and down through Ohio and into Pennsylvania. The mountains and trees were beautiful. We stayed with the Andersons in their new home in the mountains, which was on the top of a whole mountain. They have summer homes, an airport, and a golf course all on top. It is very, very beautiful. Andersons are the brother and sister-in-law of Ruth Andrews, who was our park manager at Dundee, Florida. We didn't see much for farmland or people out in the woods, although we saw bear and other wild animals, the towns seemed to be full of people just the same. Wal-Mart and everyone else were there in Lockhaven, Pennsylvania.

October was harvest time for soybeans. Also it was time for the North Central University board meeting. This was an exceptional meeting. I was given special recognition for 20 years of service on the board. I had been appointed to the board while our friend, Dr. Don Argue was President. Under his administration, the College was able to acquire several adjoining pieces of property expanding the real estate to seven acres right in the center of Minneapolis.

Now with our friends, Dr. Gordon and Diane Anderson, and Paul and Kim Freitag in control, the University just keeps expanding into another large office complex building to be adapted to fit their needs. We have seen a large six story high-rise go up, and now the Chapel is ready to go under renovation for an expanding enrollment. At the partners banquet they presented me a plaque and gift for 20 years of service and let me address the crowd of 500 people. What a challenge! Our friend Mike Shields was banquet speaker. Getting ahead of Mike on the program was a first for me. We worked with him on a Bible College in Argentina, where he always beat me to the chow line. It was a thrill to be able to present Dr. Gordon Anderson a check from the Liechty family to the University for $50,000. This was another banner year in our efforts of giving.

"Let us not grow weary in well doing
For at the proper time
We shall reap a harvest
If we do not give up"
(Galatians 6:9).

If there is anything I would like to stress, it would be that everyone needs that walk "out behind the barn," where it is just you and Jesus, and you can talk to Him.

"Jesus said, Ask and it will be given
you; seek and you will find; knock
and the door will be opened to you"
(Luke 11: 9).

The winter of 2005 finds us back in Florida. It has been an eventful year. We began our year in Sarasota with all three of our children coming there too. They brought our grandchildren, David and Jackie. Also visiting us were Todd and Jolene and

Noah Sjostrom. They also had their nephew Ben along. All of these children were a lot of fun and made our time go fast. We attended two of the cousins' breakfasts and had a great time with the cousins for Christmas dinner at Kauffman's home.

After the holidays we returned to Dundee to our home that had been hit by two of the four hurricanes that hit Florida in 2004. Our good friend, Jim Bennett, had done a lot of repair work on the house. In the storm we lost screens in our screened in porch. Wind took all the skirting away and blew out a bedroom window, shattering the drapery. The winds also tore our front porch off the entrance to our home and blew it out into the orange groves. We never saw one piece of that porch anywhere. We had inside floor damage from water raining in and roof damage from wind and rain. We were thankful Jim had taken care of all of this.

Jim and Carolyn Exner have been our guests that week. We enjoyed a tour through Solomon's Castle, attended an evening at the Bill Bailey music convention in Lakeland and played Dominoes and Skip-bo. What an interesting week! Paul Freitag also stopped by and beat me by two strokes in golf. We will have a rematch when I get back to North Dakota. Ha!!

Our first major trip in January 2005 was with Priority One directed by Joyce and Sam Johnson. Sam is a friend who grew up with us in North Dakota. The five day cruise took us to Coszumal, Mexico. Along with us were Silas and Martha Liechty, Norvel and Arlene Johnson from York, North Dakota. We were all based in Florida at the time and drove together to Tampa to board ship. Dan, Sam's brother, was on this cruise also. Dan gave me some good ideas about writing books. He encouraged me to get going on this book. On the ship we ate a variety of food like I have never seen before, all very good. We slept, read, and played games.

The purpose of the cruise was to raise money to build Bible Schools in Romania and Russia. We were glad we could be a part of another worthy cause and donate funds to this cause.

The Luis Palau President's conference and the Book of Hope rally were both held in February on the east coast of Florida. What great refreshing messages, reports of thousands turning their lives over to Jesus. What fellowship with the greatest people on earth. The reports were so inspiring we just couldn't help but dig deep and give donations to each of these ministries.

We began our trip back to North Dakota on March 10, 2005, driving a 1996 Dodge minivan which we had left in Florida several years ago. We always flew back and forth each year, and now with 120,000 miles on the minivan it was time to take the old faithful van to North Dakota and trade into something newer. We headed out making our first stop with Donna and Larry Sjostrom at Niceville, Florida. We spent the evening and night there while looking at some hurricane damage in that area. We traveled on to Gulf Shores, Alabama, and spent a few hours with Karen and Harold Schultz. There we also looked at hurricane damage and enjoyed a delicious fish lunch.

Leaving Gulf Shores we drove on to Houston, Texas. Lots of good and some tense moments in Houston. The city is large and the traffic is wild. I figure we were just 18 inches from an accident every mile in and through the city. We arrived early afternoon, rented a motel for the night, took the room keys and went to look around town. We saw an advertised doll-house that Fern wanted to see. We drove without an address for an hour and a half hunting for this doll-house, only to find it was locked up.

Our main objective in Houston was to find the church of Joel Osteen. We had an address, and finding it before dark, a lady at the parking lot said Joel would be speaking that Saturday night. We stayed and enjoyed the service. People came from everywhere. Some walked, some had old beat up cars and some cars were newer. Although it was Saturday night, the 4000 seat auditorium was full. After the service Joel invited all visitors to join him behind the platform. It was nice to talk to him, shake his hand and also take a picture with Joel.

Now to go back to our motel, the innkeeper said the road out front was route 90. We proceeded down that route only to find that our motel was not there. I took out the motel key looking for the phone number, but that was missing. As we started driving, looking where the motel might be, we got farther into the dark part of Houston. I didn't dare stop and ask directions as nothing but dark and dingy bars were open. People in bars often look blurry-eyed and under the influence of alcohol. I just don't speak their language. It fakes me out. Fern was all but in tears. I was scared and very uneasy about the whole thing. We were lost. I turned the van towards up town and found a motel of the same kind we had rented. The manager got on the phone, made several calls and located where we were registered. We got back to our motel at midnight and crawled under the covers. We were relieved!

Next morning we headed our van toward Dallas. We stayed with Cris and Jeff and the grandchildren for one week and visited Jeania and Larrie. We went through the huge three-story aquarium. We had Easter Sunday dinner with Jeania and Larrie.

Monday morning we turned north toward home (Jamestown). We stayed overnight in Kearny, Nebraska, planning to look at a farm near Kimball. I had corresponded with Mr. John Snyder since October 2004. It was the right sized irrigation farm I wanted, an area that could grow corn and sugar beets all in one section. I really wanted to look at it. We had just turned west on I-70 when our cell phone rang. It was Dede Edstrom informing us that her mother, Fern's sister, Sylvia, had passed away.

After the call we turned back north to get home for the funeral in Minneapolis on Friday. Getting home Tuesday night, we regrouped Wednesday, repacked our bags and left Thursday for Minneapolis. Morris and Lillet Sjostrom and Paul and Marilyn Gage (Fern's sisters) rode with us to the funeral and back.

On Memorial Day weekend 2005, the mayor of Jamestown, Charles Kourajian, at our church, presented Jim Gackle, Daboldt Ketterling and myself each a high school diploma. The North Dakota legislature gave high school diplomas to all World War II veterans who entered Army service before graduating from high school. I really felt honored to have this diploma. Only problem now, people told me maybe I could go get a real job.

Soon after seeding time, Kevin Hollar, my friend and irrigation equipment specialist, and I made a fast trip to Kimball to look at the farm we missed coming home earlier. We made a cash offer on the farm, but by this time the farmer decided not to sell. I still know the Lord has something for us in Nebraska. I awakened one night in a somber mode thinking about my calling and a deep sense of responsibility came over me. I went into tears realizing I needed help. I cried out, "Jesus, Jesus help me, Jesus help me." I wept myself to sleep. In the morning I felt the load was lifted. It was like a fresh new start; I was back on track again.

Now this time of year, early spring, we had traded for new combines, something we had done on an annual basis the past six years. Jamie Beachy, who ran our harvest operation the past three years was still in line to go harvesting again. During the winter months, Jamie would go to Indiana to find work. This past winter he found a girlfriend, decided to marry her and stay there. In April he told us he wasn't coming back to help us. What do we do with new combines?

Another problem facing us this year was the Minnesota farm. We had the farm rented out to Aaron Johnson, a potato farmer. All was well and good until Aaron took soil tests and discovered the previous farmer had put down a chemical on one-half the farm that potatoes would not grow through. Now what do we do with the other half of the farm?

Our two options were, either try to get another renter, which would be cumbersome as the bad soil was on various parts of the farm, or farm it ourselves 130 miles from home base. Aaron said he would plant the good ground if we planted the other. We decided to plant our half to soybeans, but who would do the physical work? We needed a miracle.

As I wrote before, I never worried about obtaining hired help. That was the Lord's part to arrange, if we were to continue supporting missionaries, churches, colleges, evangelists, and other charities. I can recall many people would come just at the right time to fill a position on the farm. Following is a list of people the Lord had provided through a period of 50 years.

June Were	Jim Gackle
Allen Martin	Allen Fercho
Amos Stultsfus	Adam Nusz
Adam Liechty	Art Duncklee
Bob Bachman	Bob Unterseher
Bill Owen	Cris Paulsen
Curtis Liechty	Darwin Verke
David Sjostrom	Doug Meyer

Doug Ely
Darryl Wileman
Edwin Nitschke
Fred Hoffman
Gerrit Van Bruggen
Harvey Wolff
Jamie Beechy
Jeff Glass
Kenis Loven
Lester Peterson
Lyle Vilhauer
Terry Ost
Todd Sjostrom
Wayne Rolle
Harold Odegard
Mick Hessler

Dan Rueb
Earl Loken
Earl Fercho
Gene Wolf
Henry Rasmussen
Harvey Loven
Jeff Liechty
John Swiers
Larry Nitschke
Llewelyn Paulsen
Merlin Trapp
Paul Liechty
Walter Bartel
Wesley Loven
Cris Paulsen

The Allen Martin family from Pennsylvania.

Seeding on the Minnesota farm.

MIRACLE 34 Now we needed help on our Minnesota farm and through the providence of God a Pennsylvania Dutchman, another Mennonite family, Allen and Bertha Martin and their eight children came driving through North Dakota looking for work. They drove west on I-94 to Dickinson, North Dakota, 200 miles beyond Jamestown, our place of business. After spending two days there, they turned around and drove back to Jamestown. Looking for a place to stay overnight they went to the Star Motel. This motel was owned by Christian people, Dick and Jean Seekins, who attended the same church we attended. Mr. Seekins brought the Martin family along to

Martin children, harvesting the Minnesota farm.

church and introduced me to Allen who said he was looking for work.

Allen and I discussed several places he had been to and the kind of work he had done. I called three references he gave, all saying good things about Allen. On Tuesday we hired Allen. Allen fit well in the farm program. We were able to rent a new quad-track Case-IH tractor, and a new no-till air seeder, to seed the Minnesota farm. This was the most modern, electrical over hydraulic, computerized, equipment available. Allen crawled on the machine and basically never stopped until the job was done.

You probably wonder where his wife and eight children hung out. We gave them residence in a mobile home in our Holiday Park Village. Although that was home, Bertha would load up the children in their custom built van along with a tent and cooking supplies and park out in the same field Allen was working in. It was fun to see the children play and run after birds and rabbits in the warm sandy soil. Bertha was able to cook up some real good meals out in the field that even I got to enjoy.

Now it was time to go harvesting. On July 1st the Martins began the harvest, moving the combines and trucks to South Dakota. Harvest there lasted longer than usual so that when he finished there the wheat crops were ready in northern North Dakota. Allen seemed to find work there until our own soybean crop was ready. We finished October 31st. Was Allen a God-send? I know in my heart he was. Things like this don't just happen. Someone was looking out for us. PTL!

On June 14th we were saddened by the passing of another sister of Fern's. Judith had been in a nursing home approximately nine months before she went to her reward. Judith was the wife of Wesley Loven, the man who helped run our farm for 30 years.

Wesley Loven 30 years   Henry Rasmussen 20 years
Two longest term men on the farm.

Wesley was very dependable, never missed a day and always on time-- an outstanding record.

In October 2005, we were invited by Dale Fagerland, our pastor's wife's brother, to attend "Our Greatest Challenge" rally in New York City. Flying to New York, taking a taxi, our hotel was right in the middle of Times Square. One trip downtown was all we ever needed. High rise buildings for several miles, traffic trying to drive seven or eight lanes on a six lane street. People on the streets so thick you could not walk straight anywhere. If you did walk, you had better cover your pockets, if you didn't want to lose things.

The meeting, "Our Greatest Challenge," was very informative of how Satan is trying to defeat the Christians, by persecution, around the world, especially in eastern Arabic countries. The Christian missionaries have paid great physical prices to try to convert people to Christianity. Although being beaten up and many times jailed, missionaries giving their own reports, were willing to continue their work in foreign lands. We were thankful the Lord gave us good crops back in North Dakota so we could help meet the needs of the missionaries by giving a good offering.

Jesus referred to needy people as having them with us always. It was our pleasure to help one of our Christian family friends, a family with three children, get out of credit card debt by setting up the debt on a three- year repayment plan to us. No interest charged here.

One day walking into our local grocery store I saw a friend checking out a full cart of groceries. Something inside me said, go pay for his food bill. I told my friend, "it's my turn to pay." When I got the bill it was over 200 dollars. The man needed help. He was feeding the children by himself, the mother had left them, leaving them to shift alone.

Another person called from out of town asking if we would deposit money in his bank account. We were glad to help. He had written too many checks and was overdrawn at the bank. The ironic part of this is that this same man a few years ago tried to shut down my farming operation. He wrote a letter to my landlord and to me stating that he wanted the land away from me. He stated in his letter "it is time for the Jon Liechty empire to come down."

"Jesus said,
Love your enemies;
do good to them that hate you
and pray for them that
despitefully use you." (Matthew 5:44).

One more time Kevin Hollar and I got into our 150 Ford truck and headed south through Nebraska, Colorado, Oklahoma, and Kansas looking for one more farm. To reach my original goal,

Nebraska Irrigation Farm.

we have Nebraska and Oklahoma yet to pursue. Kevin is a good driver and has a good eye for irrigation farms. All I needed to do was to enjoy the scenery.

We are right at the end of year 2005. As of this writing we have made offers on two Nebraska farms. Hoping something will come together. I knew the Lord had a farm for me in Nebraska. At the end of this writing we were able to purchase 320 acres of irrigated ground in Nebraska in 2006. Kevin and I did take a serious look at an irrigation farm in Oklahoma, I tried negotiating a price, but that is yet to come.

"See it is to believe it;
believe it is to see it." Joel Osteen

I wrote earlier in chapter thirteen about a man named Ben who hit rock bottom, he had lost about everything. Ben has taken on a new attitude about life and God and maybe about us. He was a wheeler dealer but no time for God. First time I approached him about not working on Sundays and going to church he said he didn't believe in that stuff.

As time went on it got to the place where a mortgage company sold us Ben's last 3000 acres. Ben's son and grandson came to us for help to keep farming. They said unless we helped things were looking very bleak.

Now they began taking notice there may be something to Christianity and maybe a better way of life. I had many good conversations with the son and grandson about taking time for God. The son said he began talking to God every night before going to sleep. He also began attending a small country church. This is a church I could recommend to anyone. Some of the grandchildren have girl friends from good charismatic churches and are enjoying their times there.

I was cautioned by bankers and friends that I could lose money, I figure if I can win this family over to Christianity it will be worth the risk. I have had good talks with Ben as we rode tractors and combines together. I asked Ben when he was going to start attending church. He promised me he is going with me when I get back from winter vacation. Ben has seen a difference in his son and grandchildren, he is thinking seriously.

MIRACLE 35 Early in the spring of 2007 Fern and I made a large pledge to donate to our local state family camp grounds. Getting closer to the time to pay I was wondering where to go for money. One ordinary day my secretary, June, walked into my office, asked me, did you pay that $40,000 note twice? No, I said. Well, said June, you deducted it twice from your check book. What a surprise, there was most of my pledge laying in my account.

MIRACLE 36 Fern and I have always been adventures and aggressive, 2007-08 was no different. One nice summer day in August 07, 2007 I asked Fern if she would go with me to Colorado to look at a farm. Yes, I don't want you to go alone, she said. We left Tuesday morning, got there Wednesday, looked at a farm. Bought one section, 640acres, and returned back home by Friday night. We had just signed a contract one hour before another buyer came around to buy.

In November I was awarded a trip to Hanover, Germany. Hosted by Howard and Brian Dahl and Amity Technology, we attended a huge International Agriculture equipment show. People from all over the Western Hemisphere were there with exhibits. Spending five days there we did not see the entire show which filled fourteen huge buildings. Amity exhibited their sugar beet topper and sugar beet lifter. Also they took a Melroe field digger, an Amity soil sampler, and a Wishick disc, a company they purchased this past year. There efforts were very rewarding as they sold all the machinery they are able to build this next year.

Amity held their annual winter board meeting, in February, on Marco Island, Florida. Returning back to Texas, after the meeting, from Ft. Meyers, Florida was not good. After checking our bags and going through security we were to board the American Airlines Plane and leave at 10:55AM. After sitting a while we learned the flight would be 2 hours late.

At 11:30 we got the word that our flight had been canceled and that we need to go to the ticket counter to reschedule a flight. Now with Fern taking time to walk slowly all the way back to the ticket counter, I wound up at the end of a line of about 80 to 90 people, standing in line for over one hour. They routed us through Miami and said we need to retrieve, our already checked bags, from a room in the basement and bring them back to the check-in counter to get them on the right flight.

Fern decided to wait at the check-in counter while I go get

the three bags. Finding the bags I headed for the escalator to go back up stairs. Should I make two trips up or can I take all three at one time? Loading the smallest bag on top of another, and putting them side by side it looked like they would fit into the escalator. Starting up with both hands holding bags, it left no hand to grab the hand rail. One bag seemed to lag behind so I turned to pull up on that bag and I lost my balance. I began falling backward, land on my back on top of the bags. Laying head down I tried to kick myself down off the escalator and wasn't getting anywhere and didn't know how long it would take. Two airport policemen came running, shut off the escalator and saved the day.

The Policemen picked me up and started checking me out to see my fate. More luck and Gods help I only had one wounded hand with four deep gashes from the steps. I had no broken bones, no other bruises and no pulled muscles. I didn't hit my head on anything either. (One friend thought a good bang on the head might have helped me.)

There was lots of blood flowing from my wounded hand. The airport Para-medics came and cleaned my hand and bandaged it with gauze and tape. Now I had a club hand completely wrapped and it's so large I couldn't get through sleeves in shirts and jackets, I couldn't get my wrist watch off either.

Redressing and washing with hydrogen peroxide, applying antibiotic ointment, and colloidal silver the healing began. PTL. Luckily it was my left hand so I could print out my dilemma.

You may wonder why I get so excited about farming. Farming to me is like hunting to a coon dog. Coon dogs are trained only to go after coon. They are not allowed to run after cars or cows or horses. They aren't allowed to play with children. They are kept locked up until a coon is in site. At that time, turned loose, they go through fences tearing their ears, they go over rock piles and through water ponds, they go through mud, thick brush, and thistles. They will do anything to get that last coon.

When I heard this story I was reminded of my farming. Farming has been my prime objective in life. Regardless of age or physical means, I would like to get just one more farm. I see the end as just one more big crop to harvest, and more money to give away. I feel my faith walk, "out behind the barn" has been fortified by Genesis 8:22.

"While the earth remaineth

Seedtime and harvest

Cold and heat

Summer and winter

Day and night

Shall not cease."

Here it is 2009 and life and adventures are still going on. After reading the book, a friend of mine said to me, "the last chapter hasn't been written." He was right.

MIRACLE 37 Continuing the story of Ben mentioned on page 102. He was an entrepreneur that farmed thousands of acres, flew airplanes, including have his own personal jet, and ran a commercial airplane crop spraying business. But had no time for God.

On page 168, Bens life of excessive material holdings had come to an end. Now he and his son were looking for financial help to try to keep farming, saying unless we helped , things looked very bleak and they would be out of business. They asked if we would cash rent the 5000 acres, some of which Ben owned at one time, that we had bought, and land that belonged to his brother, who owned the farm machinery and trucks, enough to farm the

5000 acres. To finance this size operation, both their half and our half, would take a million dollars a year.

We joined into a 50-50 share crop joint venture and have done this the past three years. During these three years, I began spending more time with Ben, riding together in tractors and combines. The only thing Ben had left for entertainment was driving equipment over the fields. Ben was temperamental. One day he would chew me out, he'd say in a mad tone, "you won't farm this land next year, I'll see to that," then maybe a week later he'd come back asking me to loan him money to buy a car or a house.

While riding around on tractors and combines, I asked Ben if he would go to church with me. He said, "I don't believe in that stuff." After several Sunday attempts, he did go to church with me. I picked him up in the morning and after church we had dinner together. Surprising enough, his son and grandchildren were there too.

In the fall of 2008 Ben began showing signs of health problems. At times he would look real yellow and we knew something was wrong. He started doctoring in December and was in and out of the hospital two times. In January he went in for the last time. I called and prayed with him. A few days later I called and questioned, "Ben it doesn't look good, does it?" He answered and said "No it doesn't look good." I asked him if he was going to Heaven. He didn't know. I prayed and he repeated after me a prayer of repentance and asked Jesus to forgive him. This was a great comfort to the surviving family as two days later he died. It appeared as though he was looking into a bright light as he peacefully passed on.

Thanking the Lord for this opportunity, I feel my mission, at least this one, has been completed. Having risked at least a million dollars, the Bible says one soul is worth more that the whole world.

After Christmas and New Years 2008, Fern noticed a lump forming in her right breast. We were in Florida with family. Leaving there we drove to Texas where we spent time with Crystal and Jeff, Jeania and Larrie.

Fern began doctoring and taking tests which diagnosed it as cancer. Although we knew we wanted to take treatments in North Dakota, our doctor advised taking the first chemo shot in Texas. Two days later headed north. Into the third day of the trip, only 60 miles from home, Fern was real sick and could not eat.

Monday morning we went directly to the emergency room in Jamestown. After two hours of examination, Fern was put into an ambulance headed for Fargo. Immediately upon arrival she was put in intensive care. The doctor in Texas did not give her a follow up shot to keep the white count up in her blood, therefore she got infection in the blood. For two days the doctor did not know which way she may go, it could have been fatal.

What could or what should I do? Fern was going through delirious times seeing big men walking through the room. She also saw a man hanging up on the wall wondering what color nail polish she liked. These were scary times. I needed help. I got up in the middle of the night, the bedroom was dark, and I cried out with a loud voice, "Jesus please spare my Fern, Jesus please," I pleaded for her survival. Fern remained in intensive care for two weeks and one more week in regular care. When we returned home we began a series of three more chemo treatments. Next was the big decision. Do we have surgery? A mastectomy? On July 7th, 2008 it happened. It was a shocking day for both of us. Fern began a new style of dress procedure and needed more assistance from Jon. Man did I learn a lot about ladies apparel, I didn't know bottom from the top, we had never addressed all bumps and angles.

Last, of course, were radiation treatments...27 trips...200 miles each time to Fargo and back. At the house we were blessed with home health care administered by Sherry Bracken. Sherry's sisters Jodi and Lori also assisted part time. Now these girls are the best, they worked hard, were very dependable, and did things just like we always did, and we had a lot of fun too. Sherry on the piano and Fern on the organ, they played the most beautiful music you could ever hear.

Had it not been for pneumonia in October, we could have ended home health care much sooner. The Lord gave us the right connections in all of this.

December 15th, we left for Florida, packing suitcases, in and out of motels. Fern moved along with a walker, we traveled quite well. We are thankful for the many prayers offered by our friends on Ferns behalf and the sustaining touch of God on her body.

MIRACLE 38 Another opportunity was made available to us in October, 2008, it was the elegant mansion at 1628 Elliot Avenue in Minneapolis, which was built in 1887 as a home for the Benjamin Bull family. Mr. Bull was a respected businessman who was engaged in many businesses including farming and he introduced the first street railway in Minneapolis. The original cost of the 3-story brick and stone building and the 2-story wooden barn/carriage house was $27,000. It was recently appraised at $850,000. The building was placed in the ownership of North Central University by the generous donations of the Liechty family. Although we got it at a good discount, being investors, we did not have that kind of money lying around. The Lord prepared a miracle. Right after I made the first payment, from an unexpected source, I received more money than what the payment was. After I made the second payment, again from an unexpected source, I received a check equal to the amount of the payment. After I made the final payment, again from an unexpected source, I received an amount of money greater than my total cost of the project. I had no idea any of this money would be coming down the pike. We were surely blessed of the Lord. The mansion is currently housing the Intercultural Studies Department and the Business department which serves over 300 students in each of their major.

As long as you keep active there are always some new experiences. In February 2009 we had 1000 acres of eight foot tall corn standing in the field. I went up to Minnesota where my crew was working. Combines were rolling in a foot of snow picking off the corn ears 30 inches above the ground. Temperatures were in the freezing mode, the snow did not stick to tires or other equipment. Trucks need to stay out on the roads, so the corn was hauled from combines to the trucks with a tractor and 1100 bu. grain cart. The corn was in good condition and drier than back in October, the normal harvest time.

In the fall of 2010 Fern was feeling good and was active as usual. We started planning for our December trip to Florida. Before we could go Fern began baking cookies as usual, planning and buying Christmas gifts, and sending Christmas cards to over 200 of our friends.

We drove to Florida, all went well. One night between Christmas and New Years Fern passed out and fell on the floor. I called 911 and the Ambulance took her to the Hospital. Fern was in the Hospital two weeks. The doctors said there was nothing they could do for her and that she should get Hospice care.

We chartered a jet airplane and flew to our home in Texas. It was the last few weeks of here life where she could be with the family. The children all came over many times to spend with

Mom. We all helped cook for her, she had a good appetite right up to the last day, it was fun to help her eat. Fern and I had several discussions about her passing on to Heaven, her main comment was "I want you to go with me". Fern had both Home Health Care and Hospice Care 24/7. Fern passed away March 15, 2011 at our home in Rockwall, Texas.

MIRACLE 39 In memory of Fern, Sam Johnson and Jack Strom approached us about taking the major roll in building a fitness center at Trinity Bible College in Ellendale, ND. When I heard the price, the thought hit me like a ton of bricks. I did not have a pile of money laying round that I could just throw in half a million dollars. I had stopped at Ellendale on my way to Oklahoma and maybe to Missouri to attend farm auctions. While driving and praying, Lord what should I do, in a little while I just got the gut feeling we could do it. I didn't hear any loud voice, just knew I should do it. I decided to do all three. Called Sam, and I made a

Trinity Bible College, Fern & Jon Liechty Fitness Center.

promise to build the fitness center. I bought the farm in Oklahoma and later a farm in Missouri. The fitness center will carry Ferns name.

It amazes me how we can accept John 3:16 as a normal promise of Gods word and live our spiritual ups and downs and come back by faith in fellowship with our Lord. At the same time we stumble over Luke 6:38.

"Give and it shall be given unto you;
good measure, pressed down, and shaken together,
and running over, shall men give unto your bosom.
For with the same measure that ye mete withal it
shall be measured to you again.
Proverbs 3:5 and 6:
"Trust in the Lord with all thine heart
and lean not unto thine own understanding.
In all thy ways acknowledge Him,
and he shall direct thy paths.

A man was leaning against a high pole, his ear tight against the pole, standing there as if he was hearing something. After a few hours I thought I better check this out. Let me try it as I put my ear against the pole. I listened ever putting my ear tighter to the pole I said I can't hear anything. Oh, he said, It has been that way all day. YOU MUST LEAN ON JESUS.

A man going into business promised his Pastor and God, if he was blessed, would give 10% of the profits to the church. First year he made $1000 gave $100 to church. Second year made $10,000 gave $1000 to church. Third year made $100,000 gave $10,000 to church. Fourth year made $1,000,000 gave $100,000 to church. Fifth year made $5,000,000, went to the pastor and asked him to pray to God to undo his promise, he said he just couldn't give

$500,000 away. The pastor knelt down in front of him and prayed silently, when he got up the man asked him if he prayed to get him relief, no said the pastor, I asked God to reduce your income to a level where you can give 10%

MIRACLE 40 James Valley Youth For Christ in Jamestown, ND was in need of more room for their activities for the youth attending the center. There was room on the back side of their property to build a one/half basket ball court center. Along with the center they added handicap access and new rest rooms to the center. This project was completed and dedicated in September, 2013. The Liechty family had the honor and privilege of supplying the funds for the addition. Rather than having a ribbon cutting ceremony, I was honored to throw the first basket ball through the basket ball hoop that was covered with a ribbon.

Back in the summer 2011 attending Lakewood Park Bible Camp, as a single man, I had driven there with my SSR Convertible Chevy Truck. The youth of the camp, with a golf cart, were giving rides to raise funds for their project. I decided to give rides in my convertible to help them raise money for their goals.

I put up a sign RIDES 99 CENTS and to my surprise several widowed ladies took the ride. Among the group was Elsie Wurgler from Minot ND., the only one to over pay the rate, paying $3. I knew there was money there. This gave me the idea, maybe I should go to Minot. Our Liechty Homes having a sales and home park business gave me a reason to be in Minot and ask Elsie out for lunch. This was the beginning of a slow but successful courtship.

In December I drove my SSR truck to Sarasota, Fl. to spend time in my Time Share on Siesta Key. I wasn't sure just what Elsie was thinking until she bought a plane ticket to come see me in Florida, then I knew there was some interest. I returned back to

ND the first of April. I began seeing Elsie every two weeks. A 400 plus miles each trip and Motel stays of $300 to $450 for the week end. We did spend two week ends at Lakewood Park Camp dating at the meetings and looking over the lake and at the moon in the dark. Elsie came to Jamestown two different times and stayed with friends there.

MIRACLE 41 I was in Texas in July, flew to Minneapolis, Elsie flew in from Minot, we spent the week end with Larry and Dianne Frietag. Went to a Twins ball game, to the Mall of America, and many fine dining places plus enjoyed several great meals with the Frietags. For some reason I got the feeling Elsie thought I was going too slow with our affair. At the airport, waiting to fly out, I tried a minnie proposal as I asked her if she would marry me, I apologized, I didn't have any flowers, she said that's OK I'll take the cash. Was I ever happy as she said YES MAYBE. Next time I went to Minot I took her one dozen roses and did it properly. Now we needed a wedding date, I asked her if we could get married before I went back to Florida December 15th. We set a date of Saturday, November 24, 2012. This was Thanksgiving weekend, our children all came in early and celebrated Thanksgiving on Thursday before the wedding.

With the favors of President Gordon Anderson and Vice President Paul Frietag we were married in the chapel of North Central University, Minneapolis, MN. Had a double ring ceremony with two attendants each and Rev. Larry Frietag officiating. Reception was held in the great halls of the University.

MIRACLE 42 December 18th we left Minot on our honeymoon heading for Florida. Driving through Nebraska we stopped for lunch with our farmers there. After lunch we headed south on Hwy 183 running into a snow storm near Ansley, NE. Looking for a motel to park for the night, road signs all frozen over with snow and ice that we couldn't read, at speeds of 45 to 50 we came to a dead end in the road. I applied the brakes on solid ice, went straight off the eight foot dead end cliff. Sailing 40 feet through the air we landed in a corn field on all four wheels going through an electric fence. The Chrysler van still in motion I stepped on the accelerator and kept driving through the corn field back out through the electric fence, through a road ditch, and back up on the road. On the road we stopped to evaluate what really happened. The right front door wouldn't close, Elsie held it shut till we got to a body shop at Broken Bow, NE, where we spent the night. The right back door would not open and hood was sprung sideways and would not open. We drove all the way to Florida in that condition. When repairing the van they found a bent rear axle, cracked radiator, front bumper gone, left rear quarter panel missing and many body paint scratches needing to repaint ¾ of the body.

We are thankful we didn't have serious bodily injuries, we feel there were many Angels watching over us.

MIRACLE 43 The opportunities for giving were still coming along. In November, 2012 Pebbles Thompson asked me to go to lunch with her and Darin. Knowing somewhat of the ministry she was doing with abused children I felt there would be money involved. I turned down the lunch opportunity and soon after left for Florida. After a month in Florida, Elsie and I went to Texas till the end of March, then back to North Dakota. All this time passed and I couldn't shake the thought of turning down Pebbles. Again in May Pebbles asked to see me and by this time I felt I was arguing with the Lord about money. Again I couldn't shake the idea so in June I called Pebbles and wanted to talk, She had a vacated school property she was trying to buy, by this time she had negotiated a price well under half a million. I think my stalling may have saved us all some money. The Lord put a figure in my mind so I wrote the check.

School building purchased for Pebble Thompson's ministry.

Jon and his toys at age 80.

MIRACLE 44 Thirty days after I wrote the check a man we had never talked to or heard of made us an offer on some real estate, which we had never thought of selling, offering twenty times as much as we had paid for the property which came into mega, mega dollars. You can't out give the Lord.

MIRACLE 45 Telephone returns- in August while traveling out to Seattle, WA for a family board meeting and returning to Jamestown, ND driving through Idaho we stopped at a McDonalds for coffee. When going to the bathroom I laid my phone on the toilet paper roller and forgot to pick it up when I left. After traveling 200 miles down Highway 90 I found my phone missing. This time I saved the receipt, most times I throw them away with the trash, so I had the phone number of McDonalds. Calling back and getting to talk to a very helpful pleasant lady they mailed my phone back to my office.

In September while traveling with the Lundstroms tour bus in South Carolina visiting the 8000 acre Biltmore Estate with many shops and bathrooms I again laid my phone on a paper roller in the bathroom. Leaving it lay there and traveling three hours later again I am without a phone. After many phone calls to the lost and found department and twelve days later my phone arrives on my desk in North Dakota. Do I need a chain around my neck to tie to the phone or what?

Eighteen
EVER GREATFUL

In conclusion, I would like to give a general statement. I thank the Lord that he could use a poor farm boy, who was chided a few times, with only a 9th-grade education. I believe my success began the time I made an altar before the Lord on the ocean liner, crossing the Atlantic ocean, at sea level, asking Him to come into my heart and guide my life, YOU TO CAN DO THIS TOO. I believe we need to take the Bible literally. Jesus wasn't joking when He said He would give us the desires of our heart or that it is more blessed to give than to receive and to love your neighbor as yourself. Then too, the walk and talk I had with Jesus where I promised to faithfully give according to the way He would bless me.

In the beginning, more than 50 years ago, we started giving 20 percent of our profits away to charities. We were able to increase that both percentage-wise and dollar-wise as the years passed by. The last few years we have given up to 50 percent. We are currently supporting over 40 missionaries, churches and charities on a monthly basis and write checks each month for the same. My goals are to continue this pattern for as long as I have good health.

"It's not what you'd do with the million
If fortune should ere be your lot,
But what you are doing with the
Dollar and quarter you've got."
                              -Mickey Carter

Our blessings have been phenomenal. Our giving to missions has opened up avenues of travel into over 40 countries on five continents. We have been on boats, cruise ships, submarines, airplanes—commercial and private, large and small. We have been blessed to be able to spend about three months out of every year in Florida for 30 years. Now we sold our home in Florida and bought a home near our children in Texas. Did you ever sell something and feel like you still owned it? When we sold our home in Florida, the new owners, Lonnie and Bonnie Titus, gave us a set of keys and said come back and stay at this place any time you like. Our children are all Christians and have blessed us immensely.

"Money is like love;
you must give it away, to get it."

-Jon Liechty

I LOVE TO LIVE

Today, dear Lord, I'm 80
And there's much I haven't done.
I hope dear Lord, you'll let me live until I'm 81
But then, if I haven't finished all I want to do.
Would You please let me stay a while, until I'm
Eighty two.
So many places I want to go, so very much to see,
Do You think You could manage to make it 83?
The world is changing very fast,
there is so much in store,
I'd like it very much to live until I'm 84.
And if by then I'm still alive, I'd like to stay 'til
Eighty five.
More planes will be up in the air,
So I'd really like to stick

And see what happens to the world when I turn
Eighty six.
I know, dear Lord, it's much to ask,
(and it must be nice in Heaven)
Please let me stay to eighty seven.
I know by then I won't be fast,
And sometimes will be late,
But it would be so pleasant to be around at 88.
I will have seen so many things,
And I've had a wonderful time.
So, I'm sure that I'll be willing to leave
At the age of 89…Maybe.
Just one more thing I'd like to say,
Dear Lord I thank you kindly.
But if it's okay with You, I'd love to live past 90.

Looking back over the past 80 years, I am a blest man to have completed this book. My health is strong, blood pressure is normal, I don't think I am afflicted with Alzheimer's, but I do have a few some-timers. We have been blessed with several farming and business goals. One of my goals which started in my early custom combine days was I always thought it good to own a farm in each state from Texas to North Dakota. That would be six states. The farms didn't line up quite in that order, but the Lord gave us farms in eleven states. It might be interesting to note that in our early days of farming, a man said one-time that if I didn't like to fix equipment, I shouldn't be a farmer. Considering that, things went pretty well on the farm. The Lord always gave me hired help that could fix. I didn't need to. It goes back to proper connections. Jesus has allowed me to drive machines, mostly pickup trucks, through the fields and enjoy His great creation.

Some people judge your success by the size of your house or the kind of toys you own. How big a home could we build if we put all of our money into a house each year, rather than giving the money to charities? I like to think I'm building my mansion in Heaven. If I don't get a mansion there, it will be worth it all to see JESUS. A friend of mine asked me if I thought he would go to Heaven. I replied, it depends on what YOU do with Jesus. Everyone wants to go to Heaven, but many shy away from Jesus, I don't think it works that way.

You might say acquiring property is no miracle, and maybe not. Although the greatest miracle is the fact that we have been able to give away millions of dollars to charity while expanding our business. You won't see a miracle if you don't look for one.

"In everything you do, put God first
and He will direct you
and crown your efforts with success"
(Proverbs 3:6)

I would like to encourage you to keep good records of your giving. It's not enough to throw in a 10 or 20 dollar bill or write an occasional check for your offering. Treat your giving like you treat your utility bills. If you borrow money to pay your running expenses, borrow enough to pay your tithes and offerings too. That is your test of faith. Keep an accurate record. If you don't give 10 percent you are robbing God, (Malachi 3:8), as you start exceeding the 10 percent, that's when the Lord will look at you with favor. You must seek and pray for divine guidance as you give, so that your funds are directed to the right place. I have NOT written this book to exalt myself. Without the help of the Lord, my wife, our children, my brothers, many friends and neighbors, all of the above would not have happened. I still feel inadequate for most of this story.

> The Lord is good, a strong hold
> In the day of trouble; and he
> knows them that trust in him.
>
> Nahum 1:7

I feel I need to make one more statement, something I needed to do to play the game of life fair. As I stated before, I served in the U. S. Army with both white and black people. My children often thought I was prejudiced toward the blacks. I don't really know if I was or not. One day while praying, I asked the Lord why He had made so many different colored people. I had no more than said it when the answer came back as clear as day. He said it was for the same reason He made so many different colored flowers. God likes variety of color and personalities, that is why He made you and me. It hit me like a bullet and I knew He was talking to me. Well guess what, today I hugged the first black person in my whole life. Praise the Lord.

There are some of you guys and gals that haven't made a full commitment to Jesus Christ, you are somewhere in between faith and failure, you are on the rough road, get off the fence. I urge you, make an altar, ask Jesus to forgive your sins and let Him come into your heart and life. Your good works alone won't get you to Heaven. You can talk to Jesus like any other person. He is waiting for you. It really is the best life.

THE END

To order this book call:
701-320-3081
or write:
Jon Liechty
PO Box 690
Jamestown, ND 58402

Or go to the Barnes & Noble website:
www.bn.com